Splitting the Atma

Revelations on Yoga

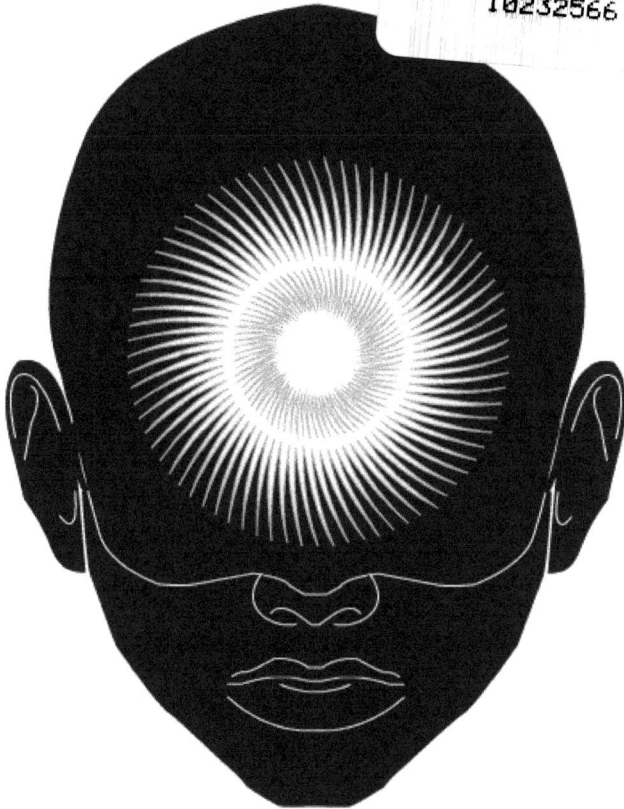

devaPriyaYoginï ~ Erinn Earth

Illustrations on front page and his book covers in Chapters 15, 16, 21 & 30 --- **Michael Beloved**

ISBN: 9780990372080

LCCN: 2020904589

Table of Contents

Introduction

Splitting the Atma: Revelations on Yoga reveals a journey of explosive spiritual self-discovery through study and practice of Yoga. The articles reflect an emergent understanding of what Yoga *really* is and how to apply it to life for the sake of literal spiritual transcendence.

What is the ATMA? It is you! Atma is the Sanskrit word meaning the *eternal spiritual person*. This person is *not* the physical body *nor* is it the psychological mind. The atma is the spiritual person, an existential singularity, - a silent, mostly subservient passenger of the subtle body (aka energy body/mental body) nature has developed through the unfoldment of evolution to fulfill its fundamental function of reincarnating from one physical body to another. The atma tumbles through this process in a mostly unconscious state, yet it itself *is* the eternal living being. Yoga is a system meant to awaken that unconscious being and enliven it to act on its own best interest.

When I say this is a book on Yoga, I do not mean that it is a journey of my progression through asana postures. Asana postures are an essential element of Yoga but are not emphasized here as the focal point as they are so much in mainstream yoga culture. I mean, we get it already. This book is also not an account of exotic travels to India or of sitting at the feet of this or that guru at so and so's ashram. I've never been to India and will probably never go. And while I greatly appreciate the incredible culture of India, likely having spent many lifetimes there, I have little desire to go and feel satisfied that I reincarnated away from it into another culture and perspective.

What this book *is* however is a collection of writings revealing my experiences in striving to understand this most advanced psychological undertaking. I practiced for years and studied the source texts as best I could until finally coming across the incredible work of Michael Beloved. Due to his canon of work including translations and commentaries on Yoga's primary source texts, I was able to *begin* to make sense of it. Over the years, through the gift of his guidance, willingness to answer questions and share the contents of these scriptures from such a profound perspective, I've been able to write these essays and share them in this book.

The state of Yoga in our world is not good. Yoga may not be what your local yoga teacher is telling you it is. Guiding you through postures in a pretty room with sweet tunes is not necessarily Yoga at all. *It depends on the teachers comprehension of the scriptures in which we find the knowledge and instructions on Yoga.* Yoga is not something the teacher makes up or discovers on their own; it is not something whimsical or new agey.

Rather, Yoga is a comprehensive platform of disciplines upon which the goal of spiritual liberation stands. Through the practice of the itemized disciplines, one's vibration increases, purity rises, objectivity grows and reality piercing perception develops. Realization of one's own participation in the cycles of reincarnation become clear and ultimately a relationship with divine beings activates. Higher dimensions are visited during deep states of meditation and sometimes even during sleep and normal waking times. Higher vision and insight are gained. It is during

Yoga meditation that many of my writings took nearly form enabling me to simply sit down and type it out after the session.

Meditation is why this book exists. The clarity of mind produced by ceasing the normal functions of memory and imagination as taught so pointedly in the Yoga Sutras, serves to allow higher functions of consciousness their time to shine. So many things can become manifest in the consciousness of the bare self (swaupa/atma) when the mind is disciplined into quietude.

The itemized instructions, as we know them today and as we knew them long ago, called the *Yoga Sutras*, are a compilation of disciplines recorded by an advanced yogi called ***Patanjali***. In this source text we find his categorization of Yoga into an 8 limbed method. In my book *Kundalini Yoga: Home Practice*, available online, I offer my own short commentary on the 8 limbs of Yoga. Like many people, I felt compelled to make comment on the wonder of the terse verses, or sutras, Patanjali coined.

And even though many commentaries and elaborations have been made *on* Patanjali's Sutras it *doesn't* mean they are not perfect *as they are*. They are perfect. It's just that they are very advanced and not everyone can truly comprehend and utilize them. They were written by an advanced entity and are stated in an advanced, concise way. There must then be the assumption that the Yoga process is meant for those who can *understand* the material as well as those who are ***willing*** to understand it.

Herein is the value of a *guru*. A guru will bring light to what you don't understand. If your guru is the real thing, you will experience one *aha! moment* after another in his/her presence due to the profundity of his/her wisdom.

In this lifetime my interest in Yoga, its scriptures, masters and deities, was immediate and wide-ranging. I wanted it all at once, but, as it goes in this dimension, it took time and patience to uncover. I studied psychology and theology in college but sensed correctly that I had barely scratched the surface of knowledge in these areas. Not long after college I was working as a direct care social worker in a group home for the mentally ill with developmental disabilities in Rhode Island and the word Yoga was mentioned to me by my boss. She said she thought I should look into it. My head shot up and my consciousness became motivated in a way I had not felt before. I suddenly felt the excitement of what I'd call 'spiritual hope', I didn't know how to describe it at the time, but in that moment I *felt* the light at the end of the tunnel.

So I started doing the exercises (asana) and started a study of the 8 limbs of Patanjali in *The Yoga Sutras*. Captivating but so advanced, I didn't comprehend much of it at first. The level of psychology I had yet to confront found within the Yoga Sutras thrilled and intimidated me. (What if I could never 'get it'?) Nevertheless, I was happy there was more to learn about psychology than what my formal western education had taught me on the subject - which almost entirely consisted of all that can go *wrong* with the mind rather than *what* the mind *is*. I certainly didn't fully comprehend the Yoga Sutras at first but it caused me to realize a philosophy so high existed in this world that very few minds dare deal with it. Patanjali's Yoga Sutras, even just the elementary translation I studied then, supported my feelings of fascination toward the potentials of one's bare consciousness (swarupa).

I felt spiritual feelings inside myself as early as I can remember but lacked guidance in thinking and living spiritually. My upbringing was a good one; my adoptive parents got along, were conscientious, educated and organized. Even so, few homes, with even the best parents, rarely provide an environment for childhood spiritual exploration and development. It was in my early twenties that I felt my philosophical wings beginning to unfold and the inkling of executing my own spiritual interests began to occur. I stopped denying within myself that existential questions existed just because they didn't seem to exist in those around me. Only then was I finally on a journey toward becoming equipped to chase down the answers to my emerging questions.

When we are children we are dependent on grown-ups for everything, therefore we instinctively acquiesce to their guidance, it's a survival instinct, going along to get along. Questioning or disagreeing with our parents is rarely a good idea and can result in the child being regarded as difficult. Despite having been brought up in the Catholic Church and school system, a place one might wrongly assume to be a spiritual environment; I did not feel encouraged to explore spirituality. And although the bible is a respectable holy book in its own right, it did not contain, for me, the ignition mechanism needed to propel me into serious spiritual awareness.

For one interested in self-applied psychology, the Yoga path provides a comprehensive approach to spiritual living for the purpose of the transcendence of the subtle body to a higher, less traumatic, less dense dimension. The lifestyle framework and behavior blueprint Yoga proposes allowed me to develop an understanding of the body and mind and how they work. I learned to organize my psyche and to make the best use of the spiritual feelings I felt inside.

At the beginning of my studies, in my early twenties, I began by making significant lifestyles changes, like stopping eating animal flesh. I also began letting go of - as well as seeking out – certain associations in my personal life. I studied and tried to impose the behavioral recommendations of Yoga, the yamas and niyamas, and attempted to apply what I understood about them to my lifestyle. I diligently practiced the stretching (asana) and breathing exercises (pranayama) I had learned at a formal teacher training in a disciplic spiritual community called an ashram - a Sivananda ashram in Val Morin Quebec.

I took my first young steps forward toward transcendental meditation experiences in those first years of establishing a junior spiritual practice. I began to organize myself internally - through self-examination, spiritual study and simplicity of lifestyle.

After years of reading lots of self-help and spiritual texts I still had not integrated the *Bhagavad Gita*, one of the three primary source texts on Yoga. Fortunately, in 2013 I read a translation and commentary by Michael Beloved. I was sort of overcome in a sense, of understanding, overstanding really. Finally I could integrate the deep existential meaning of the conversation between Lord Krishna and his warrior cousin Arjuna. It made the gift of the Yoga system, from the perspective of **Karma Yoga,** or the application of Yoga to our social actions or inactions, became stunningly more apparent than ever.

The *Bhagavad Gita* is a conversational portion of the larger epic history of ancient India called the "*Mahabharata*". Anyone who appreciates the magnificence of the *Bhagavad Gita* portion alone will miss out if not to read the full story.

Michael Beloved, and his inSelf Yoga, I consider to be the comprehensive foundation, application and explanation of Krishna's Yoga, which is Bhagavad Gita Yoga, which is Patanjali's Yoga, which is Swatmarama's Hatha Yoga – which is inSelf Yoga.

I have the work of Michael Beloved, his insights, translations and commentaries, to thank for allowing me to get anywhere near completing my understanding of this mysterious path. Yoga has been hidden, undervalued and exploited by many throughout time. The epidemic of fake yoga is at critical mass in the west *and* in the east as well. It was brought to us by swami (priest) men like Yogananda, Satchidanada and Vishnu-devananda who only gave it to us *in part,* often small part, and charged a pretty penny at that.. I strongly suspected them of only giving out a morsel of the information available and I was right. In the end, for me it wasn't any of the swami 'anandaji's' with big names in big organizations who really explained Yoga comprehensively, it was a humble yogi named Michael from Guyana.

The work of Michael Beloved's inSelf Yoga takes you through the processes expertly from beginning to end. His insights strike spiritual harmonic chords in the heart of one's heart and in the core of one's consciousness, triggering very real possibilities of divine self-discovery. It is my opinion that his insight can make all the difference in the successful development of a serious Yoga practitioner and the liberation of the soul to a higher dimension.

For future reference, here are the 8 limbs of Yoga:

1. Adherences (Yamas)
2. Restrictions (Niyamas)
3. Exercises (Asana)
4. Breathing Exercises (Pranayama)
5. Retraction of mental emotional energies (Pratyahara)
6. Effortful sublimation of mental/emotional functions (Dharana)
7. Temporary spontaneous sublimation of mental/emotional functions (Dhyana)
8. Complete Insight (Samadhi)

Also for future reference, here is a short list of certain Sanskrit words I use often in my writings but don't necessarily translate them throughout the text.

Yoga – 8 limbed system of physio/psychological restraint with the goal of self-realization and transcendence to a higher dimension. Literally translated as 'restraint'.

Kundalini – The universal and personal life force system running the cosmos as well as the physical and mental bodies. Literally translates as 'coiled she-serpent'.

Pratyahara – The retraction of one's sensual energies, mental and emotional, out of the things they are normally compelled to invest in, people, places, ideas, and rerouting those energies into one's own local psyche. The purpose is to collect all mental energy from outside things and invest it in the practice and attention to self-detail.

Samyama – Patanjali's three highest limbs. A combination of the three meditation stages in the Yoga Sutras.

The essay's in this book, *Splitting the Atma: Revelations on Yoga*, are categorized into these four portions:

- *Revelations*
- *The Yoga Sutras*
- *The Bhagavad Gita/Mahabharata*
- *Kundalini*
- *Criticism of Mainstream Yoga Culture.*

Portion on Revelations

1

How Being an Adoptee Helped Me Understand Yoga Psychology

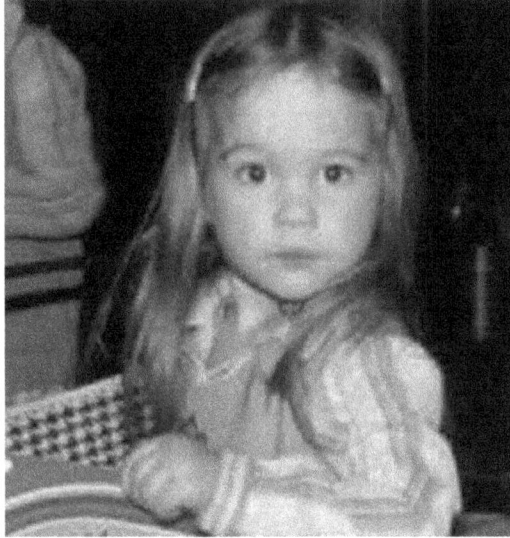

There is a similarity between my personal experience of losing my original identity through closed adoption and the isolation endured by the spiritual self (atma) while practicing Patanjali's Yoga meditation.

This meditation consists of limbs 6, 7 and 8 found in the *Yoga Sutras* and is summarized in verse two of the first chapter, *'yogah chitta vritti nirodaha'*. This means that one abandons everything it normally, naturally, understands itself to be, including the mind and emotions. Deserting all that one depends on for personality.

All of it.

Nature's design that keeps the core-self identified as the mind is interrupted, leaving the core-self to fend for itself.

It's left alone.

No thoughts, no emotions, no memories, no sleep. (Patanjali says specifically no remembering, imagining, perceiving correctly or incorrectly, and no sleeping during the meditation session.)

Nothing to relate you to the idea of you in the mind.

Separated from your natural (not spiritual) identity.

Like a newborn baby who finds itself without its mother, without her smell, sound or vibration, having the natural continuum of life interrupted.

Disassociation inevitably ensues as the infant is forced to relinquish its identity with its source reference (mother).

This article is about the rare person who is a total adoptee. Statistically we're about 1% of the population. This is a child who grows up, and may always remain, a legally classified person. Meaning, their genetic family background is kept secret from the child and its adopting family – this is meant to facilitate, for the adopting parents, the experience of a 'natural' family.

This is an infant legally surrendered by its mother, for one reason or another, and placed in a permanent foster home. While the adoptive parents have permanent legal responsibility like any other parent, the ideal is that the child will simply assume and accept, even after being made aware of his/her adoption, the lineage of the genetically unrelated adopting family.

This is a child who will never at any time during her or her upbringing receive any self-identifying information regarding families of genetic origin in these situations. An adoptee has no access to even health information and their birth certificate is sealed in a file while a new one is issued with the adopting family name.

Past, deleted.

When it came to Catholic style adoptions, children were systemically conditioned to be quietly accepting of the situation. Books available to me at that time on adoption seemed to encourage little else but a sense of gratitude that I was somehow 'chosen', even though in reality an adopted child figures out early on that they were simply the next in line. The subtler, more silencing message the child often picks up on is that it is his or her responsibility to provide a kind, loving, infertile adoptive couple the opportunity to be parents.

No pressure there!

The child is left to somehow internally manage this oddity of nature, alone, with no counsel. The secrecy of the matter creates an inner shame often resulting in an insecure, yet, introspective person.

Sounds like a decent set up for an aspiring ascetic, maybe?

An adopted child could be compared to a person living with a form of amnesia. The person with amnesia knows they must have a past, they must be someone and that they must have relatives and that the memories of those family members must be contained in the very cells of their living body.

But for the life of you, you cannot access the information.

You cannot remember.

It's hard to speculate, but do you think it would be possible for you to simply relinquish your past, surrender to your fate and construct a new identity based on the lineage of another family line?

Or do you think some of those memories and attachments might fight for survival?

I tend to think the psyche holds on.

And it is programmed to do so.

Just because physical bodies can be separated doesn't mean the same for psychic energies. We are not just physical beings. Those familial energies keep flowing between people on subconscious levels whether bodies are present or not. The psyche of the adopted child will relentlessly reach back into its ancestral past, but every single time it tries, on the conscious level it is met with a blank wall of amnesia.

We often spend many life times with and as our ancestors. Over and over we may reincarnate through one another, strengthening the attachment bonds with every rebirth.

A person seriously practicing a detachment process like yoga should be very analytical regarding what role family engrossment, meaning genetic attachment, plays in our inability to break the cycle of rebirth.

In the 1970's and for decades before, if you were to find yourself white, teenage, pregnant, unmarried and Catholic, your chances of leaving St. Whoever's Maternity Center for Unwed Mothers (where you went to find help) with your baby was slim to none. These young women's babies were 'marked' for adoption even before the birth mother had any inclining that, behind the scenes, there was a married couple very anxiously waiting for her baby.

The research and history of a worldwide baby trade has been done and made public. The Catholic Church played a large role.

Even though the baby swap era was in large part driven by the desire of infertile married couples to raise children from infancy, these parents were, in one sense, innocent in their natural and often overwhelming instinct to be parents, while also being victims of the times and the powers that be in our world.

The psychology of infertility as it relates to reincarnation is a topic for another time - suffice it to say that it is not their fault, they are not to blame. It must be said too that in terms of reincarnation, one certainly does not have to be born directly from another person to be their child. We are all interrelated when it comes to our past lives and sometimes we take strange routes to get back to each other.

To understand the psychology of an adoptee (the adopted child) as it would compare to sacrifices made in yoga, you, the reader, would have to be willing to contemplate how it might feel to have never met any of your family members. You would have to imagine growing up in a home with unrelated people. You have to imagine that you have never known, seen, or heard anything at all about your parents, grandparents, aunts, uncles, siblings - any and all genetic kin. You would have to contemplate how it would feel to have never looked into the eyes of any one you are genetically related to. You know nothing of the circumstances of your origins. Whatever happened before you were placed with a surrogate family is a void. You would have to imagine that at the time of your birth, decisions regarding your destiny were made that resulted in your natural family history disappearing from your life.

Spending the first half of my life with such a lack of self-identity reminds me of what it is like doing Patanjali's meditation which I've done many times.

This might seem like a strange comparison but bear with me. During Patanjali meditation when the core-self (atma) has no access to its familiar (family) parts (vrittis), parts that promote a 'secure' self identity (ahamkara), the core-self can go through a long period of self-questioning and feelings of isolation and loss.

For the core-self, the mental and emotional internal feelings and ideas displayed in the mind (citti vritti) *are* the old ancestors, the beloved family members who secure your place in this world.

The core-self (atma), just like a newborn baby, is interested in one thing. Identity. When we are born in a physical body we first call this identity, "Mother". At first we cannot distinguish ourselves from her. Through touch, taste, smell, sound and sight she is our first relative and our dependency on her for identity is all consuming and non-objective.

In Patanjali meditation the core self is expected to stop itself from running back to the mothering security of thoughts, feelings, visualizations, mantras and stand on its own, reaching upward, inward and outward for connection with something more. However, something more could take a long time to get to. We may have to wait a while.

Adoptee babies lack the experience of the natural continuum during the usual human experience. They are often removed from mother's presence at the moment of birth to prevent eye contact, much less physical touching. The electro-magnetic pulsations of their connected hearts are suddenly severed forcing an experience of individualization, no longer unified with the mother's vibration. Without those first inner touchstones and normal reassurances between natural mother and child, adopted babies who wait days or weeks for placement with someone to nurture them at all, can grow up feeling lost.

I grew up lacking a foundation in identity. I may have appeared fine on the outside, but on the inside I relentlessly questioned everything about myself and about families, mine and others, and the meaning of family. I studied families, siblings and their distracted mixed up obsession with each other –yet they all seemed so rooted.

As an adoptee everyday your mind wonders to those people, somewhere out there, that you came from. What happened to them? Do they think of you? You go on about life but every day you remember and feel the hidden shock that you are a sort of nobody again and again.

Although I had already done a reunification with bother sides of my biological families when I was 25 years old, when I was 40 years old I received my once classified original birth certificate from the State of Illinois in the mail. There was no name in the first name box. And only my mother's last name in my last name box. I had had no recorded first name all those years.

In 2013 I began contemplating taking a spiritual name. Often when taking a spiritual name it will start with the same letter as your given name. For me that's E. I found a beautiful Sanskrit name that started with and E and when I looked up the meaning of the word, the meaning was, 'nameless'. The message to me in this life is so abundantly clear. When it comes to our bodies and our families, these things are only temporary and essentially we're all a bunch of nobodies. It is our spiritual identity that is everlasting. This life brought this lesson into clear and sometimes painful awareness.

Eventually, my guru gave me the name *devaPriya Yogini*. Yogini is a title or category of being and deva means 'gods'. Priya means 'dear to'. So the name means "*Yogini who is dear to the gods*". With this designation I am reminded to aim my awareness not toward Earthly circumstances but toward higher spiritual endeavors. It reminds me I am much more than human.

Bottom Line

The core-self finds itself in the same predicament as the adoptee when forced to practice Patanjali's meditation. It is shocking for the self to realize how lacking in security and identity it really is. Its little spiritual arms and legs flail around in there, looking for someone or something to pick it up and give it meaning. I have a theory that this self-isolation period of Patanjali's plan causes avoidance within some people. Avoidance of meditation as well as even a deeper subconscious avoidance of accepting the existence of the spiritual self which involves taking responsibility for one's existential situation. This avoidance from my perception, promotes attachment to non-individualist ideas of 'oneness' that we see so prevalent in the mish mash of the new age culture.

In new age oneness ways of thinking, rather than taking seriously that the self exists, the ego (ahamkara) rationalizes that there is no one there, that we are all the same, all for the sake of avoiding the responsibility of being a self.

You may be able to run from your self, but I do not think you will ever be able to avoid running back into your self, here in this life, or another.

As fate would have it, I was left up to wonder who I was and I experienced the same thing when I started seriously applying Patanjali's method to my meditation. The real me was left up again to fend for itself, to find its own personhood and to bravely *yoke* (yoga) itself to something higher and greater.

On both levels, I have found out. On the physical/psychological, I did find my origins. I experienced the reunification with my bio-families.

On the existential side, through the practice of yoga, I found the true self, the eternal me that understands the greater significance of our supposed losses.

Loss motivated my interest in existential things.

Still, sometimes the eternal me feels alone and isolated in meditation. It runs back to the mind again and again for identity and I don't always reach the levels and states of meditation that I need to in order to feel connected to my spiritual parents. But I know they are always there and that sometimes you have to leave up the "old you" to discover who the "real you" is.

2

Why Yoga is My Religion

I started college as an 18 year old in 1992 at a Catholic university in Illinois. It was led by Franciscan priests - the ones who wear long dark brown robes with a cord tied at the waist. Kindly intellectuals and philosophers, they are pleasant devotees of the founder of the order, St. Francis of Assisi. They take a vow of poverty that seemed more serious than the local parish priests I was used to growing up. It was there that my studies in religion and psychology began.

One of the many religion classes I took was called *World Religions*. I was pretty psyched about it as I was more than ready to expand my personal understanding of spirituality. I began learning in earnest about the strange and beautiful religions of the world; religions that for one reason or another made their mark on humankind and continue to. I learned in this surprisingly liberal academic environment about other denominations of Christianity like Mormonism and Lutheranism, but also religions that were foreign to me like Buddhism, Hinduism, Zoroastrianism, the Metu Neter, Judaism, Islam and lots more.

It's been 25 years since college and my interest has not rested. The internet has been a magnificent resource for education and has expedited and satisfied much of my desire to know. The web is a miracle of sorts for those of us who once scoured encyclopedias, library reference systems and the yellow pages.

I like to look at religions from different angles and sides:

- What does the religion believe? How do they interpret and define the divine?
- What type of direct practice does the religion offer the entity?
- How open and clear are the leaders about the practice?
- What is the religions relationship with psychology?
- What type of evidence does the founder or followers offer in regard to direct spiritual experience?

It is popular to say that yoga is not a religion but I beg to differ because:

- ✓ Yoga is a set of specific practices for purposes of transcendence.
- ✓ Yoga involves belief in supernatural people. (See Bhagavad Gita, Yoga Sutras and/or Hatha Yoga Pradipika.)

Whether I like it or not, Yoga meets the definition of religion. A practice of the yogic religion may involve just yourself and God and the requirements. It could be you and a group of other believers, God, and the requirements. Or it might just be you and your guru, God, and the requirements.

Whatever the case, yoga is most certainly, as Wikipedia states "a cultural system of behaviors and practices, world views, sacred texts, holy places, ethics…that relate humanity to what an anthropologist has called "an order of existence". Different religions may or may not contain various elements, ranging from the divine, sacred things, faith, a supernatural being or beings or some sort of ultimacy and transcendence…"

 So why should I say it loud and proud that Yoga is my religion?

Why should I?

Probably for the same reason other people are so happy when they find their religious path to the God they love.

Something happens in the heart.

It swells with joy. It must have been what Carl Boberg felt when he wrote the poem that became the hymn, *"How Great Thou Art."*

>*Then sings my soul, my savior God to thee!*

>*How great thou art! How great Thou Art!*

Yoga is the path for me to get to the abode of the Lord who I am inherently, spiritually-attracted to. But I had to find it.

I believe that the God of *your* heart, of your destiny, attracts you, waits for you and in the right circumstances can cause you to want to be devoted, want to worship, want to serve - if you only you are informed, conscious and sensitive to Him or Her. If only we weren't so distracted by other things.

And that is really what it took for me. Eliminating a lot of distractions. Social, dietary, media, all kinds of distractions were curbed and I still work on it every day. There's always more to do but it's a joyous kind of work, the kind we are lucky to have the opportunity to explore if not fighting for our lives here on this dog eat dog Earth. I had to follow higher instincts and keep going. Keep learning and keep meditating. Keep exploring my own heart and consciousness, developing spiritual insight as to who I am and who I actually relate to.

When I look back upon my efforts as a child trying to connect with the Jewish prophet Jesus, I now realize those efforts were also instinctive, yet circumstantial. Once I was free of the environment requiring my devotional cooperation, I came to accept that neither of us, Jesus nor I, had an especially strong attraction for one another.

It's nothing personal. Yet it is.

Deeply.

I was God-less for some time in those early days of exploring. And even though I had taken on the Yoga mantle I did not yet know why. I just knew I was strongly attracted to it. As I studied Hinduism I came to understand *Yoga* as the supreme path, the final endeavor a human can execute to ascend from this place.

It was not the yoga I found in yoga studios though, but rather the Yoga in the holy books. The religious Yoga – the kind that makes the soul start to sing.

As I explored the principles found in the Yoga Sutras, it excited my inner need for advanced psychological study. Overwhelmingly. It met my needs for inducing direct supernatural experiences into my life, astral projections and lucid dreaming. It met my needs on countless levels I didn't even know existed.

After many years of teaching what I knew of Yoga, I eventually read and studied a worthy translation and commentary of the renowned Bhagavad Gita. My heart overflowed for this Lord Krishna who convincingly claims Himself as the originator of Yoga in the Bhagavad Gita.

I had found my source deity when I finally got down to serious study of Yoga and its source texts – for inevitably one finds when putting the puzzle of Yoga together that all roads lead to Lord Krishna.

For some people it is Jesus, for others it is Siva, Durga, Zeus, Artemis, Ra, Osiris, Isis, Buddha or any of the innumerable supernatural beings. I was already really head over heels for Lord Krishna when I read an abridged version of the *Mahabharata* by Chakravarthi Narasimhan. This history of Krishna's amazing pastimes with a family of great leaders, the Panavas, deepened my feeling of devotion toward him. Additionally I began paying attention to the beautiful scripture called the *Srimad Bhagavatam* which reveals the fantastic past times of Lord Krishna's childhood and young adulthood.

Intuitively, Yoga is the path for me to get to where I want to go spiritually. If that is not religion I don't know what is. Some people are scared of the word, many of them ex-Catholics like myself. But I am not scared even though I am aware of how *very* wrong religion can go when it is institutionalized by men/women. Institutionalized religion is what causes such damage to the word, not religion itself.

Therefore, it is safe to say, that Yoga is religious and it is a religion. Just because it's an every soul for itself type of practice, does not preclude it from being considered a religion.

.

3
Why Yoga Does Not Really Mean UNION

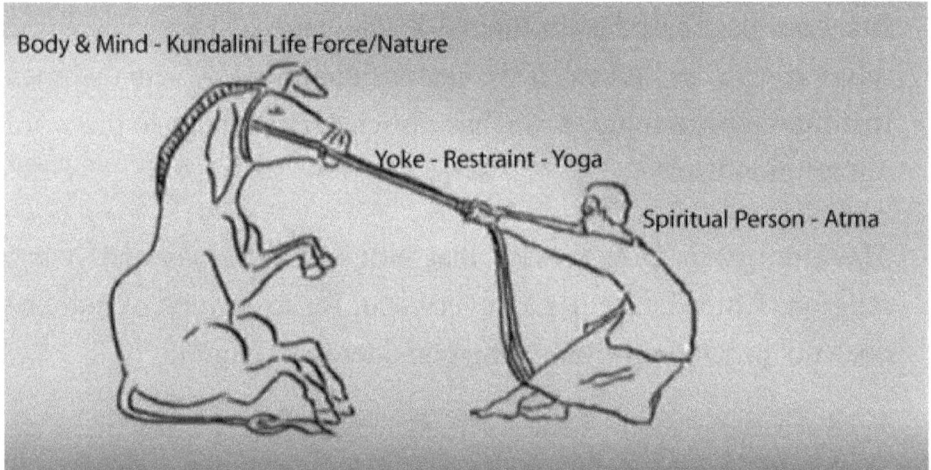

Body & Mind - Kundalini Life Force/Nature

Yoke - Restraint - Yoga

Spiritual Person - Atma

Despite 'union' being the go-to word used by popular teachers far and wide, I personally do not find it acceptable as an accurate translation for yoga.

I base this opinion on study of the three main yogic source texts:

- Patanjali's Yoga Sutras
- Bhagavad Gita
- Hatha Yoga Pradipika

If we cannot at least agree that these texts provide fundamental knowledge needed to understand the original yoga process, then we might have nothing further to share on the subject. If you can concede, or might agree, maybe then we can also agree that most so called yoga teachers and students are not studying these books.

Yoga classes are mostly about postures, not lectures, not philosophy, not psychology, not liberation.

I grew up with an English teaching mother, a known grammar-Nazi. Accurate English was highly valued and strictly enforced. What I learned from the experience is that attention to detail in language can make or break our true understanding of anything.

So what to speak of these highest philosophical yoga concepts?

The words chosen as our English translations of Sanskrit words *cannot* be vague or even slightly inaccurate, for even slight variations can cause misunderstanding. The English words are there, they are available, but if the translator is insufficient in the language and cannot find them in his limited repertoire, then his translation will be too.

Beware of anyone who tells you that Sanskrit words cannot be translated properly into English. Poor English speaking Swamis are notorious for this nonsense claim. It's such a cop out way of dismissing the student's ability to understand the essence of the Sanskrit in their own native language. It **can** be done, the words **are** there, but the translator **must** be intimately familiar with both languages.

As a yogini, I am a believer in spiritual liberation. I accept that there are ways a soul can be relocated to a spiritual environment. Yoga scriptures make it clear though that there is much to do in preparation between here and there.

Therefore, when navigating the complexities of one's personal psyche, as well as navigating the innumerable psychic dimensions it can enter into, we depend on accurate instruction through language in our holy books to get some objectivity about the whole thing. We study these special training texts because our spiritual lives depend on them. They tell the way out of the wilderness of rebirth. Imagine being given a map out of a jungle you are completely lost in. Would you want the language on the map to be super-precise? What if it wasn't? Or what if it was vague? What might happen to your efforts to successfully complete your escape?

As we all know, the Sanskrit word yoga, or *yuj*, closely resembles the English word '*yoke*'. From there, the translation somehow jumps quickly to the word union. But this is where everything is left out. How do we fit Patanjali's Yoga System in with this union idea because nowhere in his text does he refer to yoga as a union. Indeed he says just the opposite! He tells us that the bare self (swarupe) is a separate entity from the psychic and physical equipment it uses in this dimension of rebirth. Patanajali yoga requires that we pull apart what seems to already be an overly unified self.

Humans, with all our supposed intelligence, can barely tell the difference, or discern, what is physical from what is mental, much less the mental from the spiritual. During the complete restraint (samayama) meditation process, stages 6, 7, and 8, the self is forced into isolation for its own good. It is the only way for it to stop identifying with the material/psychic creation and have a chance at experiencing togetherness with a higher concentration source.

New age culture, beginning approximately with Madame Blavatsky's Theosophical Society, seemed to absorb the yoga process into its melting pot of sameness soup. There were many Indian gurus in the US at the time. Many were teaching mainly yoga postures interwoven with some oneness philosophy and proclaimed it as 'Yoga'. Their flowery repetition of yoga meaning 'union' gave great credence to the western adaptation of the word union as Yoga. It seemed and seems justified.

However, Yoga's details and stages, its true worth, its genius, and its position as the greatest of humanities psychological processes got lost in the deep pot of the new age soup. The only thing left of what some believe an archaic and overly austere path, are the physical postures. Modern culture has use for the postures in that they can improve physical health and appearance and induce relaxation. Yoga is seen, even by teachers of it, as little more than a stress relieving method of exercise.

I said it too - that yoga means union. I said it for years even though half-heartedly. After taking the Sivananda Vedanta teachers training course, I repeated this unclear and evasive idea because the Swami's at the ashram said it. At the time I believed I was getting the most thorough and accurate yoga training available in the world. However we never once dove into the books and explored the true goals of practices. How does this set the student in the correct direction? In fact his is how we end up going in a different direction than yoga, setting ourselves and students up for disappointment.   The Swamis recommended *we* read them *ourselves* but avoided dealing with them directly. Probably because they may be asked questions they would have a difficult time answering and don't want to admit how religious the whole thing is.

Yet they defeat the purpose of what a guru is really there for – **interpretation and advanced insight**.

Unfortunately, most yoga training courses focus primarily on asana. Few take students through the holy books with a fine tooth comb, which is what needs to be done to keep it honest. Instead things are kept on the surface with the use of universal terminologies that mesh with mainstream acceptability.

Finally, I will get to the real point of this article.

Why doesn't Yoga even mean union? Because.....

…Yoga actually means yoke. And what is a yoke? It is a restraint devise. What is the purpose of putting a restraint devise on something or someone? It is to restrict, control or even to force their will (nature) into some kind of submission, correct? Hostile or not, it's the reality of Patanjali's yoga.

Therefore, the word yoga means restraint. When you apply yoga, you apply restraint in some way.

In the example of a harness (restraint) placed on the donkey (nature of one's body/mind), the farmer (core self) wants the animal to submit to

his will. The farmer needs the donkey's behavior narrowed to few specific and repetitive acts. This is excruciatingly difficult and painful for the donkey at first, he resists, he complains, he cries, feels very sorry for himself and fights against the restraint. Yet, eventually, if the farmer comes back every day with the same restraint devise, places it on the animal and repeats the desired activities, the donkey is likely to surrender to its fate and resistance will end.

This is yoga.

How?

Patanjali's 8 steps show us that yoga means "restraint" - but restraint of what? First, of lifestyle (steps 1 & 2), then of material energies (steps 3, 4 & 5) and also of consciousness (steps 6, 7 & 8).

He tells us how in the Sutras.

First we restrain our social and moral behaviors. We do this and don't do that as we apply the yamas and niyamas to our social dealings. Next we are told to restrain the body, the breathing and mental attention energies. Then we restrain the core-self attention and eventually, with practice, achieve the goal of all this restraint, which is *complete insight*. **Samadhi**. Samadhi is a state of reality *piercing* clarity. The atma, the individual singularity self, has come out from under the influential mental and emotional energies which cloud his/her understanding of its existence.

It has split. Split from the material influences.

Samadhi *still* doesn't mean union. You are *still* an individual, according to both Patanjali in the Sutras (see chapter 1 verse 3) and Lord Krishna in the Bhagavad Gita (see chapter 2 verse 12). You will remain you, the atma, even once you have made it to the spiritual environment which matches your texture or vibration.

The obscured yoga process is much like the core-self (atma) itself. It has been identified with things that it is not, lost in the messy chaos of the material creation and its mish mash of non-objective diversification. If we could remove the shroud of the new age, pulling the yoga out of it like a jewel from the ground, we might see its beautiful and concentrated specialness and come face to face with unimaginable possibilities for your spiritual future.

Once again, how does this apply to our yoga practice? Remember, you are the farmer, the spiritual self, the eternal person. The donkey is your body and mind - with a mind of its own and inner impulses to fulfill certain yearnings (kundalini). Sometimes it seeks pleasure and sometimes pain. It carries with it desires both passionate and inert. When applying yoga restraint techniques, we are not creating a union, we are slowly bringing our own nature under control. It is a loss for the natural person. The kundalini loses its grip over the self. The atma has taken the kundalini through a submission process that will eventually result in yogically desired *insight*, the highest *insight,* which can be applied to comprehend the incomprehensible. Relieving the anxiety of the unknown. This is samadhi.

Yoga restraint brings the 3 parts of our reality; physical, mental and spiritual, under the gun of a tightly controlled lifestyle through close self-monitoring of who we socialize and emotionalize with, the quality of our food, exposure to media, who we have intimate relations with and who we make deals with. If we practice yoga, we restrain from lying, stealing, coveting and harming. We assert will power over our own physical and mental bodies and restrain them in postures and exercises designed for chemical and psychological purification. The more we restrain (yoga) from what influences us physically and emotionally, causing us to make non-objective, impulsive decisions, increasing our karmic debt, the more we are able to pay off the bill and move on to the next highest possible dimension.

I didn't get into yoga because I am a former dancer or gymnast or because I'm a hippy. I have no interest in being anyone's fitness instructor or life coach. I have had a fondness throughout this life (some might say obsession) to find out what yoga is and how it works, down to the most-minute detail. I've done little with the last 20 years but search for the meaning of Yoga. This has required a lot of time alone because workshops and retreats are not my thing. Reading, writing, meditating, contemplating, dreaming and reading some more are. I needed to know for myself. Not for anyone else. My interest is selfish. I have considered my relationship with God as the primary motivator for continuing the study.

In conclusion, what I have found to be true through the wisdom in these holy books is that yoga is complete and perfectly set in stone. It is an un-dissolvable pebble, whole and perfect, within the new age soup our cultures so stubbornly adhere to. It's our choice, each of us as supposed 'yoga' enthusiasts, to decide if it is worth reaching down in there and pulling it out. It will set you apart. The culture will not make it easy, but this is our fate and these are our times.

To accept the true yoga one must reject the water-down revision of it and deal directly with the reality of what it requires – this is challenging enough without the added hostility and resentment you may receive for not being part of the charade, but maybe you can do it.

4
Freudian Psychology and Subtle Body Anatomy

I notice the word ego used often in modern culture, especially in the new age movement. It often seems that if a person speaks in a certain tone, with a certain authority or from a certain vantage point, they might be accused by a listener of 'speaking from the ego' or some similar statement. I've witnessed this happening in groups and on written forums.

I've wondered, what is the nature of this common accusation of ego-mentality? Does it make serious sense or is it non-sense?

In college psychology courses students are introduced early to the infamous Austrian psychiatrist Sigmund Freud, who divided the human psyche into three parts. This article aims to compare, or associate, Freud's three developmental parts with certain developmental parts of yogic subtle body anatomy that may be discovered while working the yoga process or another discipline.

The three parts of the psyche Freud identified are:

Id, Ego and Super Ego.

The three parts of the yogic subtle form I will be associating them with are:

Primal Life Force (Kundalini), Intellect (Buddhi), and Core-Self (Atma).

In this comparison the "*id*" part of your personality is the primal life force, in Sanskrit called the **kundalini**.

Present in past live and in between bodies while in an astral environment and s and present right now in your current incarnation, this psychic energy is primitive and instinctual. The id is driven by survival and immediate gratification of wants and needs. If needs are not satisfied, the result is anxiety, fear, tension.

Easily we can associate Freud's id portion of his system to the yogic concept of primal kundalini energy found in the base of the spine which is the operator-engine of the body-mind complex in the yoga system. In this context the kundalini or id is the causal energy behind the eventual development and sustainment of the intellect.

The '*ego*' is the **intellect**, in Sanskrit called the ***buddhi organ***.

As I see it, if a person accuses another of speaking or acting from 'ego', what they are technically saying is that the person is speaking or acting from intellect. Is it really a proper insult to accuse someone of using their intellect? (Possibly the insultee should just thank the insulter.)

According to Freud, ego is a development of the id. It rises up from it, develops from it as we pass through progressive stages. As a child matures out of infancy, it begins to understand, through this natural development, that not all of its desires are going to be met, much less in the timely fashion the id demands. The ego becomes a natural limiter, a smarter, more socially appropriate expression of the primal and demanding, desire fulfilling, self-centered id.

Last and most important in the structures of the self is the highest self itself – what Freud called, The Super Ego. In yogic terms I relate this part, in part, to the Core-Self (Atma). Like the spiritual self, the superego works in contrast to or in a sort of opposition with the drives of the id or kundalini.

The superego should also be looked at as a further evolution of ego intelligence. We can see that intelligence may develop an even higher capacity for what we might call 'conscience', or the ego-ideal.

Here is the basic breakdown of my idea:

Id = Kundalini primal life force located in the base of the spine

Ego = Buddhi intellect organ located in the subtle front of the head, forebrain area, the frontal lobe.

SuperEgo = Atma, the spiritual person, who, through use of a developed intellect becomes aware of itself and its own highest ideals of self-hood, found in the center of the head space.

5
Helen Keller and Yogic Meditation: Intelligence in the Hands

The other day as I sat in meditation I realized my left hand fingers themselves were hankering for some guitar strings on them. They desired to feel the painful sting of the metal strings ricocheting through the nervous system of the body, calling on all the other parts to get in on the action.

Sometimes the body will crave a pain when there is the promise of pleasure involved.

Paradoxically, sometimes the body will crave pleasure when there is the promise of a pain involved.

It goes both ways because creation is weird like that.

So I thought to myself, *"Why do my hands themselves want this experience? Why do my hands have a will of their own right now in this moment when I am trying to meditate?"*

I caved quickly, abandoning the meditation, to see what would happen upon fulfillment. I picked up the guitar which was only a few feet away (which probably had something to do with my fingers being distracted as the fingers can sense. I realize that I should remove the instrument from the place I meditate as it is an influence) and I let the fingers play a minute. Then I put it down and continued meditating. Now fingers became quiet, even gracious for the relief and I forgot about them.

There was a tiny new connection made between me as the core-self (atma) and the psyche; a tiny new understanding that we are working together - not yet independent of each other - and that as the process of liberation is carried out, I won't always be cruel toward the body's simple desires.

I thought of Helen Keller and her hand communication and how her hands embodied her intelligence and remembered an article I wrote a few years ago on the very subject.

June 2014

Practice Report:

Thoughts in the Hands - Helen Keller

For some time I have been aware that the position of my hands can make a big difference in my meditation.

Many times I find that I separate my hands to cut off what seems to be their distracting association with each other.

I've been a little confused about why this happens, why does it even matter where my hands are, together, apart? Should that really be so important as to have influence on meditation?

Recently I may have found an answer about why my hands touching during meditation can be distracting. Putting two and two together came to me in the form of a seemingly sudden and random re-interest in Helen Keller and her hand language.

As Americans we all learned at least a little about the iconic Helen Keller. Born in 1880 she was completely normal and began speaking words at 10 months.

At 19 months she contracted something like meningitis at 19 months. The disease left her permanently blind and deaf.

After that she was a wild animal of a child and spoiled by her ill prepared yet doting parents. She used a few hand signs to communicate basic needs such as a sign for her mother or food, but for the most part she was out of control.

The parents used candy to stop tantrums. Anytime Helen had a fit or didn't get her way, they put a piece of candy in her mouth and all was well for the moment. During meal times she was allowed to eat freely off of everyone's plate...with her hands!

Her *buddhi*, or intelligence organ, was functional on a basic level but did not have the eyes or ears as physical equipment to work with in this dimension.

The family was suffering. When Helen was seven years old a young visually impaired teacher named Ann Sullivan was hired at the recommendation of Alexander Graham Bell.

The physical and psychological effort Ann Sullivan endured to accomplish even the smallest task with Helen - such as eating with a utensil - was absolutely super human.

By teaching her language, Ann taught Helen everything else. Without having unlocked the magic of language within her intellect and finding new pathways for routing its expression, she knew she could never help Helen.

So it became all about the hands. Helen's hands became her eyes, her ears and her mouth.

Through literally millions of repetitions, Ann Sullivan moved language, from damaged sense organs in Helen's head, into her hands.

How is this possible? How can the vision/vocal sense orbs, which are unable to operate accurately through the physical equipment, be moved to the hands?

Or maybe put more accurately extended down into the hands? It seems the same way we do anything else, through repetition, practice and indomitable determination. As well as the most important tool Ann Sullivan used, intuition.

Again, the actual physical and psychological effort the young woman made was beyond extraordinary.

Could you do this?

Could you be a woman with little hope of ever marrying, ever having children, having grown up in an orphanage yourself, could you care enough about life that you would take on a task no one had ever taken on before? To recondition a child who would never see you or ever hear you?

Anyway, through my own study of myself and my meditation practice, I realize why I often can't keep my hands together or even touching at all while meditating. Sometimes, it's fine, but most of the time, I end up separating my hands because it really, really seems like they influence my thoughts, even 'making' me think.

Are there actual thoughts in our hands? I believe there are in mine. I feel them. Maybe there is a link between thoughts in the hands and things like musical instruments. My hands have always played instruments, guitar, piano, trumpet, drum, kartels, clapping, snapping, expressing.

I realize I have very expressive hands.

They like to associate with each other. They like to think.

Sometimes my left hand likes to take the challenge that it can do a thing that normally the right hand does and vice versa.

So my hands usually have to be separated like two ornery children who just can't stop paying attention to each other and creating dramas.

This morning during meditation, I noticed that I had to move my left hand from the right, as far away as comfortably possible.

This quickly changed my meditation and I was able to finally quiet my thoughts. This has happened to me time and time again but I am just now understanding that it's a real thing.

I hope you will take time to refresh your knowledge of Helen Keller and Ann Sullivan, two superhuman females who unlocked one of the greatest potentials of the human psyche.

6

Queen Victoria: A Unique Study of Kundalini Shakti

We see the divine feminine show up in the physical world in spectacular ways through specific Earthly females of great status and influence. We observe vivid forms of her through activities of women who seek or even inherit great power. These Earthly creatures are prototypes of certain aspects of supernatural females.

There have been countless physical women of power in history and time will continue to generate more. To name but a few;

Nefertiti, Cleopatra, Joan of Arc, Sojourner, Queen Elizabeth, Hillary, Beyonce, Oprah, Allred, and one of my all-time favorite characters – Queen Victoria, Queen of England, Empress of India.

Queen Victoria is a good study on the incarnation of a certain type of divine kundalini mother energy. She's the type of mother who is non-objectively controlling, completely self-absorbed and regarded as super special -to herself and others. She has only her own emotional survival requirements at heart.

Constantly sexually aroused, Victoria produces numerous children she really doesn't want, indeed she finds repulsive. She is obsessed with and quite demanding of her male counterpart, Prince Albert. Albert, the perfect consort, loves her with a reciprocated obsession, also ends up leaving her prematurely by dying young. After abandoning her with of all these children, Queen Victoria holds the country in the palm of her depressed hand, excessively lamenting her dead husband for the remainder of her very, very long reign.

She makes the lives of each of her nine children a living hell until one by one they liberate themselves her desperate grasp.

Sad, because that's us. We are Queen Victoria's children.

The very nature of kundalini is the Queen of England and we are each her loyal subjects. As subjects we are not designed to use minds of our own, to think independently as an *eternal individual self* - separate from her. Modern oneness culture and non-dualistic (advaita) belief systems work perfectly with Mother Nature's design to keep us children entranced. It seems that unless one finds individuality away from her, despite her, *because* of her, there she will be, again and again, in the form of another body, at the end of every road.

Do you really want to live in your mom's house forever?

Or can you admire your magnificent mother but from a healthy distance? Distance developed through yogic detachment practices? Detachment - a condition of consciousness where she cannot reach her emotional anxiety energies into the fabric of your personhood.

We can maintain respect for the eternal wonders of nature, of material creation, but as a spiritual person, an ***adult*** spiritual person, one does not have to be bound to it, by it, forever tumbled through creation and recreation events involving entire universes as well as personal forms – forms of material energies one really doesn't control but is surrounded by as the *body* and *mind*. These physical/psychic body forms use spiritual energy like gasoline, until the gasoline realizes that it is being used, exploited, and it starts to wonder what it itself actually is. It does not understand itself to be gasoline. It does not understand itself as a potent spiritual something who needs to contemplate itself, unrelated to the sequence of events evolving around it.

Queen Victoria man, she's a trip.

7
Bound by Two Bodies
(Thoughts on Physical Existence)

I am not *only* bound to a physical body - therefore when my physical body dies I will *still* not be free of material nature. Why? Because I am bound to *another* body - and I will continue to exist in that body when the physical one I use is dead.

That body I will continue to live in is called the **subtle body**. It is made of matter less dense than the physical body.

Unlike the physical body, the subtle body is difficult to get away from so to speak. You can't just kill it off the way one can a physical one, it isn't mortal in the same way as the physical.

In other words, the subtle body is difficult to exist without. It's hard to get rid of in terms of spiritual liberation from using material creation. It's part of material creation.

Could it be that the only way to be rid of the subtle body is to wait until the dissolution of the so called universe when a dissolution-ment of everything including the universal subtle energies occurs? While the subtle body program of taking physical bodies over and over is carried out relentlessly?

This must take inconceivably long periods of time.

And just because the universe dissolves and I have no subtle body will I still identify as myself? Will I have self-awareness? Will I then be free? Depends on how I define freedom I suppose. Yet surely one could logically conclude that without having developed the atma (spiritual person) one *may* become a nothing when there is no material creation to live in. One may become a blank to oneself. One will exist but no identity (In Sanskrit this is regarded as **sat** but no **chid;** existence but no knowledge of it), no consciousness – until the universe starts up again and the atma is pushed through yet another long evolutionary tradition of matter meets spirit where matter always seems to dominate the game of identity.

For some souls liberation dawns upon the mind and disciplinary mystic methods like yoga are appropriate. In this way freedom is believed to be earned through detachment, through subtle body purification leading to transit out of the wheel of birth and death.

We are not just bound to the physical body. No, it's ways more complicated than that.

What do you think the mind is? It is the subtle body you're using right now. It's using the physical body, animating and controlling it, but it is not the physical body.

The mind exists on a mental plane, a vibratory level somewhere above the physical vibe. Its energies are designed to animate the meat bodies for as long as it lasts.

Another word for astral is subtle.

Another world for subtle is psychological.

Another word for psychological is psychic.

(But none of these are the spirit or spiritual existence.)

Nature is both the physical and the subtle.

One less dense than the other.

Consider dreaming.

You are still in a body when you're dreaming.

You still feel like you.

Yet your physical body is laying there asleep isn't it?

So which one is 'you', the one sleeping or the one conscious in the dream?

The direct use of the subtle body is experienced when we dream....but....

...not all of it. A good portion of that subtle life force has to stay in the physical body to run the physical functions. Reflect that if you eat a lot before bed, get drunk, watch a scary movie, anything you do is in the body mind complex and the kundalini is going to have to deal with it – this leaves a limited portion of the subtle energy for use in dreams.

This is why we retain little and comprehend little in dreams. We don't normally realize how lacking in clarity we are in dream states and just go on like it's no different.

That is how much objectivity you really have about what dimension we exist in.

Look how quickly we forget physical existence when in a dream!

Why is that?

The mind is easily confused is it not? Therefore it makes sense that when the subtle body passes from the physical one there could be some mental confusion, panic and grasping during the event.

Yoga practice and preparation is going to help keep us focused and on point during the passing. And since it is inevitable, we can either leave ourselves vulnerable to panic or we could go ahead and plan for it. Get ourselves into the right frame of mind through conscientious living and purification of the anxious energies in the mind.

For some, in a very serious, non-superficial way, *Yoga is the plan*. Krishna's instruction and Patanjali's eight steps *are* the plan for not losing our heads when it's time to let go of the physical body.

Only focusing on the physical part of you causes unnecessary trauma. Being atheistic won't pay off in the end when you find yourself without your physical body yet still alive despite. We cling so much to the physical body because, in terms of reincarnation, they are hard to come by. Availability is limited therefore the psyche and un-developed atma don't like to let go of them. But the subtle form is long term. It will be there with you, practically *as* you, for a very, very long time.

Anyone genuinely interested in yoga liberation will have to become very familiar with the contents of the subtle body and work toward its purification.

In closing, it's important to discern what nature is and what spirit is. Understanding the subtle body is the first step toward understanding the self within it – the spirit within the nature.

So remember, its nature over here on the physical side, and its still nature over there on the dream side

Its nature over here on the physical side, its nature over there on the meditation/transcendental side.

Its nature over here on the physical side, its nature over there on the disembodied side.

Spiritual paradise is outside of material creations. It is a place where anxiety does not exist. To be there, we must have no further need for relationship with any material energy.

With our true identity realized and secured through austerity and proper association we become Sat-Chid-Ananda.

To read more about the subtle body and its psychic abilities please see my book, *Sun Gazing – Aura Seeing & Naad Hearing,* available online.

8

Seeing Beyond the Vedas; Are Advaita Vedanta and Yoga the Same?

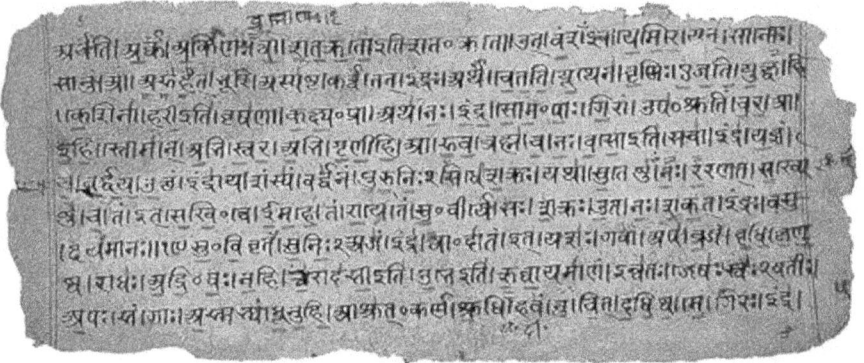

For thousands of years the individual existence of the soul has been debated.

Even with the awareness of reincarnation which involves physical and subtle bodies, the question of a spiritual body still haunts us –

Do we exist eternally as an individual spiritual entity, or not?

Is the spiritual self, the I-self-consciousness (atma, not ahamkara) that some discover in deep meditation, is it real?

Or is individuality, aka personalism, an illusion explained away by the claim that the one and only thing that actually does exist has, by its own accord, split itself into pretender units of pseudo-individuality?

Impersonalism

Advaita Vedanta and Buddhism are unconcerned with the search for the ultimate individual self or even for a personal God. They are concerned with realizing that personal identity itself is not real and being consciousness of this knowledge is the end of trauma.

Buddhism has a goal of non-existence all together, while advaita vedanta has the goal of merging with a differentiation-less universal energy which is not at all a person, but an energy. Buddhism goes so far as to be totally unconcerned even with the deity (gods) aspect of spirituality, while Advaita Vedanta tolerates traditional attention offered to deities but ultimately doesn't believe in the true existence of such deities.I became aware of this oxymoron while attending teacher training at the Sivananda Ashram.

Advaita Vedanta, often associated with the renunciate Shankara, would have us rest assured that the end of all knowledge lies in the abstract poems and rituals found in the Vedas. That what exists exclusively is a singular force. That the appearance of what seems to be the unique, individual souls we experience, is unreal. Not just temporary mind you, but UNREAL. Some even call it ignorance.

These older philosophies have made a startlingly popular reappearance current day in the form of New Age oneness concepts, revealing a hybrid type of generic popularity within the new thought 'spiritual' culture.

Personalism

Now then, what about the road less travelled, Personalism?

The personalist sees the creation and accepts that it exists. This person understands that just because something is temporary does not mean it isn't real.

They perceive the eternality of the material creation, the Mother, the Prakriti.

This person accepts that spiritual energy is something altogether separate and all together in combination with the material energy.

This rare individual (see *Bhagavad Gita* 7.3) at least from the perspective of yoga, who is interested in Lord Krishna's yoga method, is often conducting secret and self-specialized mystic actions (kriyas), aggressive breathing purification (pranayamas) and spiritually dynamic meditations (samyam).

This seeker develops a supernatural perception necessary to perceive that within the supreme effulgence of what appears to the masses as atomic oneness, there are actually kingdoms and spiritual peoples, together, in full individualized consciousness within that spiritual environment. These souls are not absent from it consciously - as one would have to be, that is, unconscious, if one accepts that only oneness exists.

Advise on How to Figure Out What YOU Believe:

There is nothing wrong with being an eternal someone, it isn't egotistical or arrogant.

There is nothing wrong with being no one, it's an imperative, unskippable developmental stage in the transmigration of the spiritual self.

But meditation is key. Self-inquiry is essential.

A regular Patanjali based yoga practice should eventually reveal where you are with things for now. Continued, persistent meditation in the location of the core self, within the center of the subtle head space, should reveal if you exist or not. It very well could be that some of us exist and some of us just don't, depending on many things including what tools we are endowed with to perceive such transcendentally mysterious things....

If you decide you don't exist, there are many options; Advaita Vedanta, Buddhism and all of the new age paths are popular and appropriate for aspirants of almost all levels. You'll be welcome at festivals and hippies will think you are the sun itself. This Earth dimension is designed for oneness soup consciousness. Obviously, we live in a Petri dish of basic ingredients. We are conditioned to put others first and to not be self-centered.

However, for those that find that someone in there, a self, a spiritual person, things might not be so easy. You won't be going to any festivals or making friends with New Agers. I've personally found that oneness folks are surprisingly easy with the insults if you don't agree with them. You can expect to be called arrogant, egotistical and ignorant for believing *you* exist. Yet, no need to despair, you are probably already an introverted loner and luckily, we don't have to rely only on the lovely primal poetic musings of soma drunk Brahmin - who's hold on the spiritual monopoly of the times benefited them and their families beyond measure.

Personalistic Yoga is the path least taken and as far as I can see, the highest path exclusive to those souls cited by Lord Krishna in the *Bhagavad Gita*, Chapter 6 Verses 44-47 (Michael Beloved translation) He says:

> *"Indeed, by previous practice, he is motivated, even without conscious desire. He, who persistently inquires of yoga, instinctively sees BEYOND the Veda, the spoken description of the spiritual reality. (44)*
>
> *From a steady effort and a consistently controlled mind, the yogi who is thoroughly cleansed of bad tendencies, who is perfected in many births, reaches the supreme goal. (45)*
>
> *The yogi is superior to other types of ascetics; he is also considered to be superior to the masters of philosophical theory, and the yogi is better than the ritual performers. Hence be a yogi, Arjuna. (46)*
>
> *Of all yogi's the one who is attracted to Me with his soul, who worships Me with full faith, is regarded as being most devoted to Me. (47)*

Concluding Thoughts

Yoga is something special.

It *isn't* Advaita Vedanta. Indeed Lord Krishna reassures us that yoga *transcends* the Vedas.

In closing, I'll point out that Vyasa, grandfather of the warrior Arjuna, split the Vedas into four sections. Author of the

Mahabharata, he himself called *it* the fifth Veda.

Why would there need to be a fifth Veda? Because the Vedas hadn't ended with the four books or even with the poetic Upanishads.

Just as Christians developed *beyond* the Old Testament, yet it is dear to them, we as genuine YOGA aspirants are required to develop out of the primal discoveries of the Vedas.

Again, Krishna, Lord of Yoga, in the *Bhagavad Gita* Chapter 2 verse 12, makes it more than clear in his conversation with Arjuna what the nature of the soul is:

> *"There was never a time when I did not exist, nor you, nor these rulers of the people. Nor will we cease to exist from now onwards."*

Patanjali comes along later and codifies a perfected syllabus.

If you meditate long and well, you may come to one of these simple conclusions:

- I am nothing.
- I am the Universal Principle Itself, no less, there is none other than me.
- I am me, you are you, God is God, and we are together in this thing.

Each of these conclusions is a developmental stage.

9
The Separateness of Silence and Sound

Silence is always there.

Something that I've discovered from meditation practice is that the sound of silence is always present -even if noises are present within it.

I've practiced listening to the silence, focusing on the silence, and noticing that it remains available and detectable even when other sounds are there too.

It is a paradox, but a handy one. How can oppose-able things be present at once and yet distinguishable as still separate from each other - even something as subtle as sound?

Because, even in this creation of atomic same-sameness, we find that everything is separated by a barrier. It's the reason that when someone jumps off a building they don't go through the ground, they splat onto it because their own bodies electromagnetic barrier has run hard up against the electromagnetic barrier of the ground. Nature causes them to remain separate even at the expense of destruction.

There is separateness inherent in all things - even if there is also togetherness.

Sound is no different.

In meditation I can hear the empty vessel of my own psyche - and I can also project my hearing outside my body and detect the silent, empty vessel of my environment. Even when there are sounds being made.

In a way, a glass full of water can be seen, as yet, still empty. The glass and the water are never really one; one is just temporarily containing the other.

Think of ocean water. It appears that the salt and the water are one. But if you take a bucket of that water out of the ocean and allow the water to evaporate, you will see the salt is still independently present from the water. And the water is independent of the salt.

Close your eyes and think of the ocean water and just focus on the water alone, as independent from the salt. Then shift your mind to the salt and focus in on the essence of the salt only.

Keeping the eyes closed, now do the same with sound. Empty the mind and focus first on the container of silence that is your inner world as well as the local container that is your outer world.

You can detect sounds within the container, but understand that they are not the container itself. The container remains itself.

This may seem complicated and it is not the easiest thing to explain. However I thought I would try because it has helped me in meditation.

The best thing about locating the silence and focusing on it is that one discovers that silence itself is a sound. It resonates and has super subtle vibrations and can lift consciousness upward.

Heightened awareness can lead to the great experience of the most-high inner sound, NAAD sound. Naad sound is the inner, unending, supernatural OM.

10

mindFULLness or mindLESSness?

I see so many advertisements on "mindfulness" meditation. No offense to its promoters, but it always sounds just horrible to me. To think that I would sit down in meditation only to be filled by, surrounded by, comforted by the mind? Can I really depend on my mind to fill me with peace? Is it not it itself that is causing a lack of peace? The last thing I want to do when I go into a serious meditation time is to be mind-full. The mind is what I am trying to get away from, to become less full of, less influenced by.

It is a different matter if one needs to sit and contemplate. This is a different sort of meditation that could more accurately be called, contemplation. Sitting down to think on something, sort out a personal issue, is one thing. Disciplines of introspective study can help with meditation in the long run, but there is a clear difference between the two activities.

As for actual meditation, yogic style, we are left without the mind to be full of. Instead we become full of a self-awareness beyond the constant urges of the mind. We begin to have an inkling of ourselves *without* the mind.

Patanjali's meditation requires mind*LESS*ness. The mind is required to sit down and shut up. Like an ornery student in a classroom.

I am mind***FULL*** when I am working. I am mind***full*** when I am driving, speaking, acting. The mind is always on call, always on duty. It's how we live in this world.

However, it is within Patanjali's samyam meditation, limbs 6, 7 &8, where I finally force the mind off-duty and into a state of quiescence. Then, I, myself, can actually sense myself and not just more stuff that fills the mind space.

In mind***ful*** meditation one would sit in the midst of the overwhelming influence of mind, become the mind, contemplate and examine the mind and ultimately remain identified as the mind.

In mind*less* meditation, the core-self (atma) is separated

(kaivalyam) from the mind stuff and given the opportunity to sense itself as a singularity, without the mind, memories or intellect.

Mindless meditation is exactly what Patanjali was talking about: a mindless journey to the bare self and its life beyond birth and death.

11

Meditation is Like First Dates?

Beginning meditation is a little like first dates.

At first when two people decide to get to know each other, they may feel uncomfortable and anxious about it. Feeling shy, awkward and insecure are things we might all remember experiencing to some degree when beginning a relationship.

The pressure of first dates can be eased by going out in a group. Hanging out with other couples, attending public functions and group events can help people more comfortably ease into a relationship.

Group distraction takes the pressure off.

However, as familiarity deepens, eventually the pressure lessens and the desire for privacy develops.

Those initial necessary distractions to ease anxiety through socialization become unnecessary and should be left behind for the sake of deepening the relationship at hand.

Meditation is similar.

The two parties meeting up are: the mind/psyche (manas) and the core-self (atma).

The two can meet up in the safety and easy distraction of a group meditation if needed. Many people start off this way.

Western culture is saturated with group meditation opportunities, comfortable places for a new relationship within yourself to have its beginnings.

But eventually, just like with people, as things become more serious, the advancing relationship will need privacy, solitude and a willingness to focus exclusively on each other. Issues will naturally arise. Troubled times may be experienced. Elation, discouragement, misunderstandings and revelations will be experienced. (Keep a journal to not forget them!)

The point of our yoga practice is that the mind and the core-self get to know each other. This relationship is studied and reformed throughout the entire execution of Yoga. It is not just a one way street. It is important for both of them to know each other.

The core-self needs to understand how the mind manipulates it. The mind needs to learn that the core-self is the ultimate, yet hidden, self and that its job as the mind is to serve this spiritual superior. That it should provide the self an environment in which to grow. The mind accepts that its function in Yoga is to allow a changeover of authority to take place as the self becomes empowered through the practice. The mind comes to trust the core-self and can release itself from its insecurities and clinging ways.

It is a truly humbling and submissive experience for the mind.

While the core-self (atma) remains trapped in this creation and is subjected to the use of material elements both physical and subtle (prakriti), if it is interested in *Yoga* it should make effort toward yogic understanding of the relationship between the mind it uses and itself, the core-self.

It is part of our yogic training to unravel the mysteries of the relationship between the mind and the self.

So.....what is the ultimate course for these two entities trying to get to know each other and come to terms with each other?

Patanjali's Eight Fold Yoga Program!

The **yamas** and **niyamas** will straighten up your social behaviors and help you to organize yourself as to what you should and should not do culturally, out in the world. How you will conduct yourself in relationships.

The **asana** and **pranayama** will clean out the psyche, empty chemical and psychological trash, straighten up and organize the mind and its contents so that it is in the best condition to meet up with the core-self, who is shy and underdeveloped at first.

It's a complicated relationship and power passes back and forth between the mind and the self along the way to redemption.

Pratyahara (sensual energy retraction) keeps us internally interested in the study and progress of this relationship between the mind and the self. Pratyahara keeps the core-self self-interested and psychically interested rather than focusing on external and redundant distractions - including group meditation events.

Patanjali's sixth, seventh and eighth limbs of Yoga are the breeding ground for the resolution of the relationship being established.

As the two come to understand their role with the other, a healthy, fixed and controlled (yogic) core-self should emerge as the dominant entity, guiding the mind along smartly with the spiritual program requirements. (See Patanjali Yoga Sutras translated by Michael Beloved.)

Through study of our holy texts, like Patanjali's *Yoga Sutras*, *The Bhagavad Gita* and the *Hatha Yoga Pradipika*, we become aware of the nature of the relationship between these two.

With the learned cooperation of the mind, with its support and submission, the core-self can develop itself, using the irreplaceable platform of a controlled mind to reach higher and higher into the dimensions of creation, cultivating relationships with higher beings and energies, eventually liberating itself from the use of material (mental) elements.

All of this is done in the privacy of meditation. In the privacy of one's psyche only, not the psyches of others.

Once we get past the initial discomfort of meditation, we can leave behind the group of psyches that only serve to keep us distracted from real meditation and move on into the depths of the relationship we share with material creation.....and shed it if that is what we find we want.

The point is, don't remain attached to group meditation experiences. The natural progression of getting to know the self, yoga style, will require that you abandon the ways of a beginner.

12

What is Dharma?

Dharma is how you must live your life – in order to live 'righteously'.

It is the best way you can conduct your daily activities, to live a morally effective life.

Karma, or action, is why you must live your dharma that certain way.

Karma is how you got yourself into your particular fix.

And karma is complicated; it's a mixture of your own actions, the actions of others and the prerogative of deities particular to your personal existence.

Dharma is even more complicated then.

Because as you act (karma), you alter your righteous lifestyle requirements (dharma).

So you have to be very careful, very conscious.

Very self-aware and gently - but relentlessly - self-scrutinizing and self-correcting.

Keeping track of both. Karma and dharma.

It's like spending money on a credit card. Every time you make the action of spending (karma), your balance debt changes. Now, the life you must live in order to pay off that debt has altered (dharma).

From a multi-dimensional perspective, viewing a person comprehensively as a chemical and psychic conglomeration of the current and past lives, dharma is understood as what is necessary for that individual to do in this world, through activity or non-activity, in order to succeed in making spiritual advancement.

Dharma means we have to live a certain way in order to mature as a spiritual being. Dharma requires disciplined lifestyle for refined self-awareness, otherwise dharma is easy to lose track of.

The requirements of our individual dharma's are set by nature (but not necessarily supported by nature), and by divine forces.

So how do we figure out what our dharma is? How do we tap into the unseen reality of these forces? There don't seem to be many maps leading out of this dimension.......

......but I have found one.

And it has great reviews and a reputation for success.

The eight armed Yoga meditation process, in its highest stages, with continuous simultaneous application of all eight parts, reveals to us our own existential situation and how we should advance forward, upward, toward higher living environments by living our dharma, our duty, in the here and now.

Requirements that when complete will, in a sense, fulfill the wills of nature and God, balance the forces within and allow for an opportunity to slip away from the traumas of this undesirable material creation (3rd dimension) and find oneself eligible for entrance into a higher dimension, or ultimately, into the world of spiritual consciousness. The 'chit akash'.

An example of a person's complex dharma is that of the epic warrior Arjuna from the most important of Hindu texts, the Bhagavad Gita:

If your dharma is like Arjuna's in the Bhagavad Gita, your direct dharmic instruction to you from God Himself was to kill many of your own cherished (yet corrupt) family members in a great violent battle. Arjuna the greatest warrior didn't want to do it. As prepared as he was, he was uncomfortable with his own dharma, as many of us often can be. And without the supernatural support of Lord Krishna, Supreme God of Yoga, Arjuna would likely have abandoned his required actions and dug himself deeper into material creation and further away from his dharma.

As many of us do every day.

So to make a long story short....

If spiritual liberation from this dimension is what you're looking for I can tell you that I've not come across another method more comprehensive than Yoga.

For most spiritual liberation isn't even a thought, especially since so many people are trying to become gods on earth - not realizing they are *here* because they are *anything* but.

Exploiting material nature is a great past time for most who incarnate here. Do as thou wilt eh? According to the top level mason and influential Satanist Aleister Crowley?

But Yoga isn't about getting the most out of *this* world - it's about the glorious *self* and its salvation *out of here* to a higher, more refined plane.

An awakened core self, atma, knows this is not its ultimate abode. That this place is not its home so it seeks its dharma and makes moves to be released from this dimension. It doesn't find fulfillment at this level.

On the other hand, an awakened and unchecked kundalini (urge system) feels quite at home here and seeks to exploit the environment as much as possible - come what may.

If our dharma, right living, involves activity in society, we do it for purposes of self-purification, for living the dharma, for burning the karmas.

Not for redeeming greatness here.

In Yoga it's every soul for itself.

As Yogins we're making serious arrangements toward checking out of the hotel matrix here in 3D.

We'll leave the Earth as we found it and allow Mother Nature to continue on her way. We don't have the power to change it, as much as we'd like to think we do, we don't, we are peewee entities with little free will, therefore we must utilize what we have available to us to transcend it and sense out a higher dimension to strive for.

There are better places to exist, but we often must make efforts to get there.

Dharma, right living, is the key!

13

Be Anal About Your Meditation Not Your Mat!

A true short story about being a Yoga teacher.

About a year ago I had a student show up who also calls himself a teacher, a 'master teacher of teachers' no less. Even though he came to my class he seemed reluctant to cooperate with my instruction by going through the motions wearing a sour attitude on his face. At the end of exercises and breathing, when time to meditate, the class is very specifically instructed to put the mats neatly aside and head indoors. As usual, the entire class did as they were instructed, simply put their mats aside, headed indoors and took their seats for meditation.

This teacher man stayed back, hemmed and hawed, worrying about his mat, folding it slowly, carefully. He paced back and forth looking for a place to put it where no one or thing would bother it.

As I am waiting for him and the class is waiting for me, his friend whispers to me..."He's anal about his mat." I whispered back, "Why is he not anal about his meditation?"

The friend shrugged his shoulders.

I continued waiting, he eventually made it in to the meditation room but the damage was done. His misplaced focus not only sabotaged an opportunity for himself, but now he will have to deal with the karmic responsibility of disrupting the meditation of others and nullifying the efforts they made to prepare themselves for the event.

Meditation is the most important event in a yoga class. Everything a yoga teacher does to purify your body and mind during the exercises and breathing is supposed to be designed so that you having a fighting chance at a successful and spiritually progressive meditation. This is clear in the Yoga Sutras, we cannot change it. However, many overlook it and end up teaching yoga as if it is nothing but a glorified stretch course. Rarely, if ever, explaining the higher techniques, the goals and the challenges.

Your yoga mat is not a person, so don't personify it. It is not special to your practice any more than any other tool. Don't make believe it provides you with any security. It's not your friend. It is a tool. If someone takes it, get another.

YOU are a person and Yoga, the whole 8 stage process, is meant for your liberation.

Stay focused on the real goals, don't miss out.

We can use anything as a mat.

Portion on

The Yoga Sutras

14
Pratyahara
(Sensual Energy Retraction)
The Leg Up of Yoga

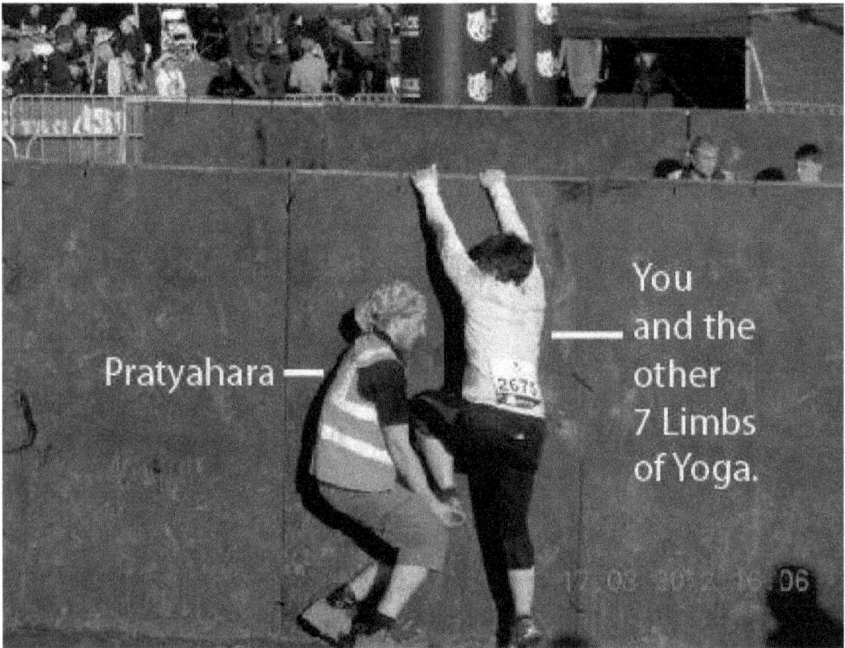

Success in practicing the eight limbs of Patanjali's yoga is quite reliant on limb number five.

In Sanskrit it is called **Pratyahara**.

In English it means to literally *retract mental and emotional attention energies out of the things they are usually compelled to invest in and to redirect those energies into the 'self' for the purpose of self-examination and purification.*

So first of all, who exactly is it that is doing this pratyaharic retracting?

It is the core-self, the spiritual person, in Sanskrit called the atma, who is performing the retraction.

The core-self is the one who the entire system of yoga is addressing, awakening, enlivening, developing and ultimately, liberating.

Without the atma, there is nothing to be done in yoga, therefore pratyahara keeps us self-focused, self-interested and self-referenced so as to not abandon or fake the practice.

Through the retrieval (pratyahara) of attention energies, the core-self is empowered to take on the job of yogically managing its local physio-psychic environment (the body and mind) and to begin the big job of clearing away and learning how to avoid karmic (action) debt.

Pratyahara becomes a deep type of introspection, a super sensitive kind of special attention I've only found in the advanced psychological practice of Yoga. In fact once an individual has been working away at the Yoga for some lifetimes, he/she might come to the conclusion that the act of pratyahara is the real champion in the quest for liberation.

Why?

Because in yoga it's all about being careful about the choices we make. From our social behaviors, to asana, to how we perform meditation, every action and non-action has consequences. These consequences are the equivalent of debt. Yoga is meant to distance the core self from its investment in material creation through what Patanjali describes as '*the cultivation of non-interest in the mental and emotional energies (cittavrtti)*' and to, even while acting in the world, eliminate the debt.

Patanjali says in chapter 1 verse 12 of the Yoga Sutras translation by Michael Beloved:

> *"By not having an interest in the mental ideas and emotional feelings, you may develop the power to stop their influence".*

By putting the core self to work and accepting the responsibility of itself and its fate, this willful action of internalizing attention can give the self (atma) the leg up it needs to manage the other limbs of yoga practice that come before and after it, which are:

- Social engagements and restraints (yamas, niyamas parts 1 & 2) - we constantly and unconsciously increase karmic debt through unnecessary interactions and by avoiding necessary interactions. Pratyahara brings our attention to necessary lifestyle adjustments that serve our practice of inner detachment even when we cannot outwardly. In the *Bhagavad Gita*, Lord Krishna explains very clearly that by maintaining yogic inner detachment to the outcome of worldly events, one can act in this material creation but not be indebted with the usual consequential energies (phalam).

Mystic exercises (asana part 3) - must be done with the special focus and the mental cooperation needed to allow the body to move itself in just the right ways to access all the parts of the psyche for clean out. Asana are not the same for each person therefore each person must be self-focused on a super-sensitive level in order to cull out the mystic cleansing benefits of the postures.

- Breath infusion (pranayama part 4) - without pratyahara, we will not pay yogic level attention to the intricate job of distributing oxygen while extracting heavy gases (mostly CO_2) and psychological waste energies. Pranayama must be so efficient as to be the bridge one crosses into heightened awareness and mystic insight.

- Progressive Meditation (samayam parts 6, 7, & 8) - If we don't engage pratyahara we will never cross the barriers of mind and body into real, transcendental, direct line meditation. The type Patanajali expects from those who accept his standard.

We have the most serious job to do in Yoga.

If we are studying our Yogic scriptures we understand that this job is to take control of ourselves, connect to higher energies and beings and to do our best to make ourselves ready and eligible for transit to a higher dimension upon the death of the current physical form.

If the psyche is dirty and clogged up it will continue to reincarnate right where it is or even into lower species or dimensions. Pratyahara helps us avoid this and to keep our focus on spiritual goals.

Again, in Yoga we believe that the only way we can transcend out of the current dimensional level is to clean out the psyche (aka astral body or inter-dimensional energy body) by changing out the energies within it through:

- lifestyle management (steps 1 & 2)
- yogic exercise (step 3)
- yogic breathing (step 4)
- internalized yogic attention (step 5)
- samyama meditation (steps 6, 7, 8)

During a session of asana and pranayama, we engage pratyahara so that we do the best job of getting out heavy, depressive, anxious, passionate, hyper energies from the body/mind, while simultaneously infusing oxygen throughout, establishing a clean environment for the sake of the core self and its ability to sense itself during meditation.

We use powerful, serious breathing exercises (pranayama) to make this happen, but it's the pratyahara that makes the pranayama and asana work how they should for real yogic success.

Pratyahara makes the whole Yoga system work, the axis that keeps it all together.

During application of pranayama the mind energies are brought inside the psyche. This takes mystic will power. No more thinking about this and that, or feeling emotion this or that. During repetitious yoga practices the mind is trained to be ready, cooperative and to work for the goal of the core-self, which is self-realization and acquaintanceship with divine beings during meditation *in this lifetime*, as well as future relocation to those divine places and people in our next circumstance. The mind learns to sacrifice itself and even find contentment under the existential direction of the core-self.

With us and at work at all times, pratyahara is the willful action of keeping control of what the mind does, where it goes, what it seeks and when.

Pratyahara keeps us in a non-distracted state of clarity and focused strong on our spiritual goals.

15
Separation Yoga

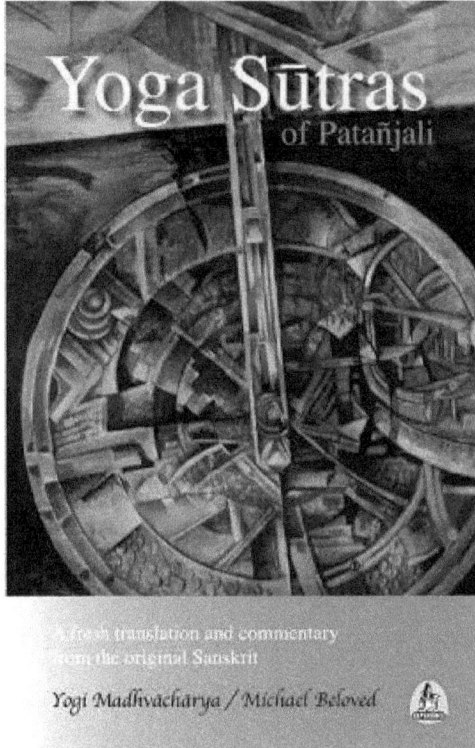

Before I came across a really well translated commentary on Patanjali's Yoga Sutras, (after years of getting nowhere with Satchidanada's version) even the profoundly important second verse didn't have a lot of impact since I did not know how to separate myself from the mind.

I didn't really know who I was separating the mind from.

Maybe this a problem for others too, whether they know it or not, when it comes to applying Patanjali's most important verse.

The second verse in the first chapter of Patanjali Yoga Sutras Michael Beloved's translation says:

"Yogah Chittavrtti Nirodhah" - which in English means:

> *"The skill of yoga is demonstrated by the conscious non-operation of the vibrational modes of the mento-emotional energy."*

The problem is (and maybe part of the reason these Sutras are neglected by yoga culture at large) that I could not truly understand verse two until I studied a proper translation and commentary on the verse and started meditating seriously, daily, routinely, abandoning visualization. I had to sense out serious ways of performing internal mystic actions that separated me from the influence of the mind surrounding me on all sides.

I think of these actions as "separation yoga" The word for this separation Yoga in Sanskrit is *kaivalyam*.

I find that the only time I spiritually feel somebody, like the so called atma, like the so called core self, like some centralized unit of existence, is when I truly experienced the reality that I am not the mind or anything stored in it.

The mind is a separate devise, it is and contains the 'chittavrtti', the mental and emotional fluctuations.

Yet I am seated in the center of it as if someone put me in the center of a radio and now I have to sit there, hearing and seeing the world through it.

But if we are to practice Yoga, Patanjali Yoga, we find internal ways to separate from the surrounding devise – and this is what the second sutra is and further, what samayama is (Patanjali's steps 6, 7, & 8) - the sequential practice of separation.

However, if one does not believe in the self, if one believes in non-individuality, then there is no one to be conscious of anything in this non-operation operation and Patanjali's instructions are useless, especially when you consider the very exciting next verse, verse three, which states.

"tada drastuh svarupe avasthanam"

"Then the perceiver is situated in his own form."

'Drastuh' is the perceiver and 'svarupe' is what the perceiver is when situated (avasthanam) in his own form!!!

During Patanjali meditation, it is important to abandon thoughts. Sometimes I am literally in there saying 'no' to whatever thought attempts to gain control of the core-self's stable consciousness. It's so fragile. When the core-self is at the beginning of this difficult practice, sometimes all it has is the capacity to squeeze out a firm, NO! - each and every time a thought approaches.

It's a start and we have to start somewhere.

Jai Shri Patanjali, thank you for leaving us a map out.

16
Yogic Non-Reactivity: Can You Do It?

Bhagavad Gītā
English
✓ Easy Read
Michael Beloved / Madhvācārya dās

Yogins are not people under an impression that by declaring devotion to a certain god that the soul will be taken to heaven upon death.

Yogins do not rely on rituals and superstitions to appease deities in order to gain their favor and be magically lifted out of the material creation into a heavenly world upon death.

Yogins DO sense that there is work to be done and that no matter what deity you find yourself in allegiance with and whatever ritual you perform, the work must still be done.

What is the work?

The nature and instruction of our work is found in our inspirational yogic texts; *Bhagavad Gita, The Yoga Sutras* and the *Hatha Yoga Pradipika.*

In the *Bhagavad Gita* Lord Krishna tells Arjuna the warrior prince, who is facing a bloody battle he suddenly doesn't want to fight, this:

> *"When the embodied soul goes through the death experience while under the dominance of the clarifying mode, he is transferred to the pure world of those who know the Supreme.* (14.14 - Michael Beloved translation)

This 'clarifying mode' is a state of no anxiety.

This is a state of consciousness and psycho-physical non-reactivity.

Imagine in your worst most challenging moment acting with total clarity and calmness?

This seems an extraordinary thing doesn't it?

Considering how reactive we all are, even over very simple things and interactions.

Are you able to not react?

By 'not react' I don't necessarily mean to *not act*. What I mean is, can you, even while carrying out necessary activities that might normally cause anxiety, stress, increased heart rate, remain in a psych-physical condition of non-reactivity?

Non-reactivity would require control over the:

- nervous system
- endocrine system
- cardiovascular system

Have you ever examined how the nervous system operates?

Studied how the endocrine system squirts hormones into your blood stream for every little reason?

Traced the chemical source of your heart rate increase?

Truly, a yogin is not a regular person. Every day, every hour the yogin strives to stay alert and attentive to his own emotional condition and strives to keep it in the mode of clarity.

This salvages his/her ability to remain unaffected, detached, clear headed, focused on God.

A yogin uses inner psychological techniques to keep himself in the mode of clarity no matter what the situation.

The yogin leaves behind natural reactivity for a higher type of behavior.

As for myself, I'm working on it. I try to use every opportunity I get to remain aloof in this material creation but yet still carry out my duties, no matter what they may be.

It's sure not easy.

17
<u>The Yoga Sutras:</u>
My Commentary on the Profound Value of Part 2 of Michael Beloved's translation.

Standardized holy books, no matter from what background, that have stood the test of time, books like the Yoga Sutras and Hatha Yoga Pradipika, are so very valuable because they remain a fixed statement. A perfect reference. They are like pronouncements from a deity or saint, capturing the claim, the formula, in a book form. Our Yoga holy books tell us what has been saved of the ancient yogi - scribe's masterful writings on the subjects. They are an intricate scaffolding through which we receive instruction in its most concise form stated in the flow of the language of the time.

However, due to general lack of insight most of us are unable to elaborate much on the instruction given in the holy book. We sometimes become too sure of our limited interpretation. Or we fumble around with it, turn it around in our block heads with an underlying fear of misinterpreting, re-interpreting or being perceived as just not getting it.

Hence the need for an expert interpreter, a guru commentator on the instruction given from the holy book.

The deity figure who wrote the original book, shouts out a command in the form of the verses we read. The guru, in between myself and the deity figure, receives the same verse, knows (through application) what it means intimately and shouts over to me,

"What he means is this, ...!!!!!

Honest gurus are merciful to help us with this material. Lucky for students, there is a pleasure in teaching.

Gurus provide a fast track to understanding. They save our brains from the drudgery of trying to make sense of the statements in the books.

Between pages 55-77 in the Michael Beloved translation and commentary of the Yoga Sutras, we find ourselves sitting with the guru who speaks our language. This section of the book, to me, states what the guru would say to you to get you to understand what the deity or saint was saying. In Part 2 of this book, each verse is said again, not changed, but stated in a way that can possibly penetrate the psyche of the person living today.

I rely on this section of the book and it has helped my comprehension every step of the way.

Most of what Patanjali said, no matter how well stated in easy to understand language with elaboration, is beyond the interest or ability of most it seems.

The verse I have been using for my own benefit as well as reading to students at the beginning of class is on page 58 - Chapter 1 verse 34, which reads:

That abstract meditation may be caused by practicing a method of breath manipulation wherein the vital energy of the gross and subtle body is enhanced, causing the creative urges to subside, so that the higher nature is experienced.

This verse sums up what we are in for at the start of a yoga session:

- ✓ *The goal is the meditation at the end and that is said upfront in this translation.*
- ✓ *He points to breath manipulation as the cause of this meditation.*
- ✓ *During the breath manipulation the bodies are ENHANCED.*
- ✓ *Enhancement causes a decrease in one's desirous nature.*
- ✓ *At that point, when this is done, the higher nature is perceived.*

That's a good session from start to finish!

I encourage myself and students to make much effort to detect what the translator translated as "enhancements".

What do those enhancements feel like?

Where are they located?

What effect do they have overall?

What parts have I enhanced and what parts are left to be enhanced?

18

Yoga Means Control

Even beyond yoga meaning restraint it actually means control.

When you've accomplished yoga you've accomplished control of your own personal energies.

You've accomplished a control of each of the 3 parts of the self:

- Physical Part
- Mental/Emotional Part
- Spiritual Part

Whether it's just in your daily activities or in a kundalini rise or meditation yoga is control.

Restraint = Control

Remind yourself to tell them. As the conscious atma, you must tell the body and mind to be on your side. To work together for the good of the atma. To be on board.

To yoke, control, restrain together the three parts.

Even if the yoking is a working together, a collaboration, it still starts with restraint.

The yoke still results in the restraint of all three parts.

Yuj = Yoga = Yoke = Restraint = Collaboration of the Three Parts = Control.......

= Samadhi.

19
The Yoga Way

The Yoga Way is the purification not just of the body and the mind, but also of the obligations.

You have to complete your dharmic duties.

You have to complete yourself.

You have to like basically live out to your fullest potential.

Seriously, how often do people ever really do that?

That takes a real dissection of the entirety of the personality - which is kind of complex.

So the yoga way is to get the business finished, here, so that liberation can occur.

I learned this on a deeper level by reading the *Bhagavad Gita* and the *Mahabharata* where we see Yoga in action in the lives of great and small people.

We read of sublime supernatural experiences between gods and people recorded so elaborately by the author Vyasa in the Mahabharata. We learn how tricky reincarnation is and how we too must use our special Yoga powers to determine, discern, what our duties are and how they should be executed. We learn what our potentials are, to fulfill them, and to not be attached to the results of what we are supposed to do. That is not our responsibility. That it is the Gods - like Mother and Fathers - responsibly.

So we understand how yoga works by reading the Mahabharata and from within it the Bhagavad Gita conversation where Lord Krishna really breaks it down, revealing the true quality and promise of the practice.

That's the Yoga Way.

Portion on

Bhagavad Gita

20

Living in the Sea of Gunas

I remember being a little girl at St. Mary's School and my best friend and I would leave our classroom every Friday morning, earlier than the rest of the kids, to go over to the empty church and set up the music for the weekly children's mass. We played guitar and sang and we would be so off the chain excited every single week - like out of this world giddy - over being able to get out of class early, being alone in the church and the anticipation of leading the music.

Of course, we couldn't be the types to be physically bouncing off the walls (Catholic school), but inside of myself I was so excited every single Friday that we were going to do this thing, that we were going to be up there singing, we were going to giggle and look at everybody and be alive. At some point we would be so anxious with anticipation that 'fight or flight' would kick in and we would have to run to the bathroom where we would laugh more and mindlessly relish in our mood. It was so strangely fun.

But now I look back and wonder, what was I so excited about? What really was the big deal? What was happening to me? I was in a little tiny town, in a little church, a little person, a little guitar and there I am going off the deep end with this emotional excitement.

It is the same surge of nerves, although no longer all consuming, that, to some extent, I can still experience to this day.

It's called the passion mode – 'rajas' in Sanskrit. It makes you feel alive when those hormonal juices in the endocrine system are deposited into your blood stream and you feel that emotional jolt into action. We often call it happiness, nervousness, elation, anticipation.

So I was an excitable little child apparently. I mean, how could someone feel that much joy, completely sober, in totally mundane circumstances, yet be so drunk with passionate energy over a nearly nothing experience? Because that energy exists in this creation - and our bodies, minds and senses are made to make redundant use of it.

In the *Bhagavad Gita* Lord Krishna tells us that there are 3 modes of material nature. They are called **"Gunas"**:

- The mode of passion.
- The mode of depression.
- The mode of clarity.

Either you are in a mode of passion, of some form and type and degree.

Or you are in a mode of depression, some form, some type, to some degree.

Or you are in the mode of clarity, some form, some type, to some degree.

In chapter 14 of the *Bhagavad Gita*, Lord Krishna states that He is about to explain what He says is the *"highest information of all knowledge's, the very best"*. He states that once this information was realized by yogi philosophers, they went away from the corrupt material world to the Supreme Perfection.

Bhagavad Gita translation by Michael Beloved, Chapter 14 Verses 5-11 say this about the Gunas, the modes of material creation:

> *Clarity, impulsion and retardation are the influences produced of material nature. They captivate the imperishable soul in the body, O strong armed hero.*
>
> *Regarding these influences, the clarifying one is relatively free from perceptive impurities. It is illuminating and free from disease, but by granting an attachment to happiness and to expertise, it captivates a person, O sinless one.*

Know that the impulsive influence is characterized by passion. It is produced from earnest desire and attachment. O son of Kunti, this mode captivates the embodied soul by an attachment to activity.

But know that the depressing mode is produced of insensibility which is the confusion of all embodied beings. This captivates by inattentiveness, laziness, and sleep, O man of the Bharata family.

The clarifying influence causes attachment to happiness. The impulsive one causes a need for action, O Bharata family man. But the depressing mode obscures experience and causes attachment to negligence.

When predominating over impulsiveness and depression, clarity emerges, O Bharata family man. Depression rises, predominating over impulsiveness and clarity. Similarly, impulsion takes control over depression and clarity. When clear perception, true knowledge, is felt in all openings of the body, then it should be concluded that the clarifying mode is predominant.

Meditation:

Turn your attention within yourself. You're going to go in there to try and sense out each of the modes, because they're all present.

The potential is there for each of them to be dominant.

The potential is there for each of them to be FELT by you right now.

So let us start with the mode of **passion**.

Remember what it felt like when you were excited about something, nervous about something, overjoyed about something. That's the mode of passion, that feeling - that surge of happy hormone into your system.

The mode of **depression**.

Think about when you have felt sadness, depression, fatigue, hopelessness, pointlessness, lethargic, heavy, stagnant, slow minded, inert. That is the mode of depression.

The mode of **clarity**.

Think of the feeling of inner peace, balance, clear-mindedness, quiet mindedness. Think of a time you felt relaxed, steady, stable, balanced, no anxiety, no nervousness, no emotion. Clarity.

Identify the modes within you because they are all there, they are all operating you.

They are the puppeteers of your life – they are your moods.

They are the environments you enter, the repetitive rooms that the core self gets drug into time and time again and somehow has to bear the burden of the resultant debt acquired through those actions.

For a person truly interested in Yoga transcendence, this has to stop.

So as the observing self we do this inventory of what is within us -what surrounds us, what enfolds us, what protects us and what destroys us.

We categorize it, get it together, and get things in order.......so maybe we too can get to the place Lord Krishna called the "Supreme Perfection".

Bhagavad Gita Explained by Michael Beloved: An Academic Review

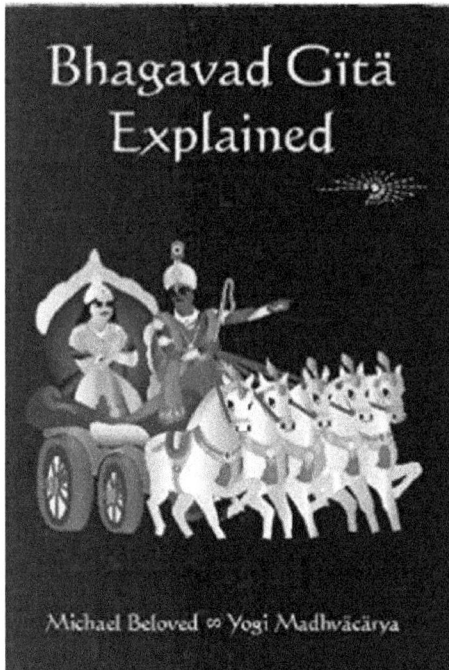

This is a review of my preferred translation and commentary of the Bhagavad Gita. Today was the second meeting of the study group held at Unity Church of Sarasota where the class decided to focus on the Michael Beloved version called *Bhagavad Gita Explained*. This book provides some unique attractions.

First, the academic layout makes clear sense to even a beginning

Gita scholar. It is clear, simple and consistent. The book is physically larger than most, biblically large. From its weight one senses that the author was unafraid to comment the heck out of the verses, providing not only the conversation at hand, but much more. Upon completion of the text and even long before, the reader has gained invaluable insight into the ways of the times, the caste system, yoga, psychology, reincarnation, devotion and spiritual advancement.

A second feature of this version appreciated, is the clarity of translation. Believe it or not, this is unique. When cross checking the Sanskrit, it doesn't take long to discover that some translators of the Gita are; too vague, overly general, and redundant. Some reveal a lack of diverse English vocabulary available to the translator. In a few circumstances we find translators skewing word meanings for sect-motivated purposes. In the case of translating Gita, one would need a universe of English words at his disposal to choose from. What was once a handful of Sanskrit has become millions of words in English. Words are important. When it comes to making spiritual progress through the application of what it says in our holy texts, accuracy means everything!

Third, the author keeps the conversation contained in the Gita within the context of the original story from which it came. This story of origin is called, 'The Mahabharata'. This is a great gift – an opportunity to understand the larger story and cultural context of the time. It is so worth it to know. We discover an ancient past, a different age – a time when the undeniably great Lord Krishna was present on Earth. A time still marked by war and conflict but also by something higher - an awareness of yoga and its power to reveal to the atma a higher existential environment. We learn that on the battlefield when a warrior trained in yoga is dying he seeks to 'go into Yoga', making his psychic transition of the physical form *without panic*. Through yogic restraint, he instead transitions consciously, with detachment. We benefit from reading of the conversations and relationships between the divided Bharatas.

Even more profoundly we are given a glimpse inside the special relationship certain characters share with Lord Krishna as he counsels and guides them through their challenges.

Although there are many differences between this commentary of Gita and others, the last one I mention here is this: the insight of the writer himself. The commentaries are stunningly informative and engaging. Anyone hungry for understanding of the Bhagavad Gita will likely find what they are looking for in these pages. Unbiased, inspiring and simply a joy to behold, *Bhagavad Gita Explained* is a gift to humanity.

22

Mahabharata:
The Magic Mushroom of Yoga

The Mahabharata is to me what LSD was to Timothy Leary…

…..what the mushroom was to Terence McKenna.

These advanced intellectuals were psychedelic activists, philosophers who used special chemical compounds, or plants, as mediums to experience other dimensions. During a 'good' trip, profound insight into oneself might be gained, glimpses into the wondrous mechanics of nature and into consciousness, revealed.

Leary and McKenna encouraged use of psychedelics because they offer dependable, non-addictive, and often therapeutic astral experiences. They felt the plant offered a merciful bypass around difficult austerities and the trickiness of yogic meditation.

They felt it was part of the development of the human consciousness.

I am like them – but in this lifetime my magic mushroom is the Mahabharata – and I encourage all students of Yoga to take it!

The experience of not just reading, but thinking about and processing the stories in the Mahabharata has enhanced greatly my inner spiritual feelings and caused insights to come about within my awareness.

I know what life *was* before Mahabharata and what life is *after*. I know what my understanding of Yoga was *before* Mahabharata and *after* - as well as my understanding of Lord Krishna.

It is my opinion that without study and assimilation of the Mahabharata, one may never understand the beautiful reality of Yoga.

What is that reality?

It is that *all* the roads of Yoga lead to Lord Krishna. One also begins to sort the fact that many of these roads to Krishna are laid by the author of of the most important of Hindu texts, Vyasa, a great yogi scribe who wrote the *Mahabharata, Srimad Bhagavatam* and many of the *Puranas*.

Books, especially scripture, are not mere words on paper. All books are filled with energy, and of course some books are filled with special energies. As yoga students we seek to find those special energies, some of which come to us only through time with the books. Ask any happy, devoted Christian, or Muslim or Jew. Any Hindu, Sufi or Buddhist - without the books, we are lost. Existence is too complex and too much work has been done and documented to take seriously anyone who dismisses the fundamental importance of scripture.

The *Bhagavad Gita* portion of *Mahabharata* is life altering on its own, yes. But the rest of the story opens up endless avenues of understanding. Energies from the characters themselves can penetrate your psyche, clear your vision, inspire your faith and motivate your practice.

According to those who know, drug trips can be quite difficult.

So can *Mahabharata*, but it's worth it.....just like that Ayahuasca diarrhea I hear everyone gets.

Portion on Criticism

23

I Am a Yoga Teacher –
Not a Fitness Instructor

When people ask me about Yoga these days I almost always correctly assume that what they think Yoga is - is inaccurate. I've found that my life and their questions are made easier if I make a few simple things clear upfront. Despite that 'yoga' is seemingly everywhere, I am nonetheless forced to accept that most people do not know what it is or ignore what it is to keep alive the false imagery of what it is not.

As a Yoga Teacher I am NOT a:

- fitness instructor

- physical therapist or anatomist

- life coach

- mental health counselor

- shaman or a healer

- new ager

- trying to make a living on it

I am not a former dancer, a gymnast or a double jointed contortionist (and if I am it is of no significance to my practice).

I am no longer a person who teaches a stretch class but calls it by an ancient Sanskrit word that I don't really understand the meaning or true importance of.

I don't have anything to prove as a Yoga teacher except that I know what I am talking about when it comes to Yoga. If I am other things, I list and teach those things separately, respecting traditions formulated and standardized by people greater than myself. I try to allow each disciplinary tradition to stand alone, on its own. If I feel to pioneer something new, I do not name steal from another tradition already established.

If Yoga were practiced and taught honestly in this world, there would be far fewer of us involved because Yoga requires the company of the self only. Most of what we do is done all alone. It is not done in groups or at festivals and has nothing to do with aerial devises, paddle boards or unicorns.

Yoga is one's own responsibility to complete; it is a serious thing for serious souls who are seriously trying to achieve future existence in a better dimension. Even if we are funny, fun-loving people, we must also be comfortable with the seriousness of Yoga.

So as long as students and teachers keep avoiding the *Yoga Sutras,* the *Bhagavad Gita* and the *Hatha Yoga Pradipika* as their sources of practicing and teaching material, Yoga will remain one of the biggest lies in our world today. These books are gurus and can be leaned upon heavily since a physically embodied Yoga guru is nearly impossible to find in this creation as it is. I have come across only one.

So I tell people - I tell them what I am not,

and I tell them what I AM:

What *am* I as a Yoga teacher?

- I am a student of the scriptures from which Yoga is told to me by its originators: The Bhagavad Gita, The Yoga Sutras and the Hatha Yoga Pradipika.

- I am aware of reincarnation and I study it. (If I have not developed the intuition for reincarnation I am not ready for yoga, much less teaching it.)

- I have studied, practiced and reached a point in my evolutionary process that allows me to confidently, accurately

articulate Yoga to others. This is what qualifies me as a teacher, not a teacher training course or some numbers behind my name.

- I assist students in the direct, safe and controlled manipulation of the Kundalini Life Force, as this is the purpose of Patanjali's step 3 and 4, asana and pranayama. Routing of the kundalini life force upward through the central subtle spine of the astral body can cause transcendental events that I am prepared to assist the student all the way through. I study the Hatha Yoga Pradipika for this mystic knowledge.

- I assist in the application of meditation, stages 6-8. I point the student in the direction of their own existential energies and allow the student to find themselves. I facilitate and encourage naad sound awareness (inner ring of OM).

- I personally execute a constant yoga practice. Yoga resides in my core consciousness at this point in my own personal evolution and I am in an almost constant state of pratyahara, meaning an internalized awareness and control of my personal energies and self (atma) consciousness

If you find that as a teacher you are attracting students who are needy, dependent and require lots of help with simple things like understanding postures, breathing, basic existential concerns, and lifestyle problems, you will waste much of your time teaching things to them that are outside of yoga practice. You will become a life coach or a counselor or a new age self-help teacher. There is nothing wrong with any of these things, but you will not have time to teach these types of students the Yoga. They will need other kinds of teachers and teachings. You might guide them toward a practice or teacher you feel is more appropriate.

Genuine Yoga students are tough, open minded, but specifically drawn toward yoga austerities because of progress made in past lives. They want to upgrade themselves mystically and spiritually and have faith in the Yoga method. They ask questions but are not challenging. They recognize and respect your authority as a knowledgeable teacher. They will see you as a means to an end, as a helpful direction giver toward achieving personal liberation.

Students ready for a real yoga teacher are already intuitively performing their own version of asana, pranayama, meditation and lifestyle reform even if haphazardly. They are already internalizing their attention energies. They are studying, seeking, trying to organize themselves. They are already aware of certain things but absolutely need the final direction, yogic clarity, grace and guidance of a teacher to put it all together and make it work. They are not needy! Don't strap yourself with fakes and hanger-on-ers! These students will inhibit your own liberation and that is not what we are teaching for!

Stand tall and be selective. It is not necessarily that the student is choosing you as a teacher but rather you are approving them, or not, as a student. Release yourself from trying to make money from it, do something else for money – something practical. Your student's genuine interest in Yoga is your payment - not to mention the graces you may receive from appreciative Yoga deities and masters.

We do not baby those who come to us as students. We believe in them as adult spirits ready to take on the greatest of challenges, Yoga's 8 steps. They are ready to let go of everything here and seek spiritual existence. If the combination of their spiritual awareness, intellect and desire is correct, they will be able to take on the complexity of yogically navigating the mind, mending it, directing it and ultimately mastering one's way out of this dimension.

As a Yoga Teacher, these are the students I deserve and so do you.

24
Will Yoga Teachers Ever Actually Teach Yoga?

Some of us are really out here trying to teach this stuff and it's hard to be taken seriously.

With so many teachers in the world how is it that the public still has so little understanding of what Yoga is?

Why do I know so many people who have 'done yoga' for decades yet have never heard of or studied the Yoga Sutras?

How come so few people involved in yoga have a serious

meditation practice or are familiar with samyam meditation?

How come I've had students who will not come to my class because I discuss reincarnation?

Yes, I'm talking about Yoga, the ancient mystic practice of asceticism, NOT groups of people stretching, de-stressing and saying namaste.

The teachings can be found in three main texts that all practitioners and teachers should know and adhere to for support:

First, the incomparable Yoga instruction Lord Krishna gave to Arjuna during the battle in the Bhagavad Gita.

Next, The Yoga Sutras of Patanjali describes Yoga as an 8 stage process of detachment, self-control, self-purification and advanced meditation.

And third, the revelatory practice details offered by Yogi Swatmarama in the Hatha Yoga Pradipika where we find incredible specifics on the 6 highest stages of Patanjali's 8 fold Yoga.

These books contain the yoga information. They contain what yoga *is*. They have what we need, we just need to understand. These texts came out of a time in antiquity when yogic power was at a maximum. As yoga students and teachers we need to know this information. If is not known a legitimate conversation on yoga cannot be had. And what a loss! Yoga is so much, so beautiful, so difficult, so enthusing, healing, enlightening - we find the truth of yoga in these texts. It is not limiting to consider the standard practice in those ancient books, indeed it is freeing to get out from under the modern redefinitions, alterations, and even distortions which several teachers standardized as yoga but which are in contrast to the ancient approaches.

Please help!

It is my observation that the majority of yoga teachers are actually teaching stretching combined with principles more related to the Age of Aquarius - and calling it Yoga. I know that most teachers, even Indians (India), offer up little knowledge of actual Yoga in its original, unalterable, super-advanced form delivered to us from the mouths of Gods and Masters. Everywhere you go, asana and world peace are the focus.

Let us not be so quick to dismiss it all if we have not even bothered to master what has already been done.

The other day, for the thousandth time during nearly 20 years of being a yoga teacher, I was asked the question: "What type of Yoga do you teach?"

I used to have my go to - Sivananda Yoga. Back in the day when I was less informed I was comfortable with this reference even though I knew in the back of my mind that they had NOT adequately explained Yoga and I didn't know why. I thought I would really learn about yoga there, it seemed the most traditional training I could find. But as usual, *even they* focused mainly on asana. So much so that as a female my menstrual cycle shut down for a full six months. I had to cut back on the asana I was supposed to be doing as a teacher for it to start back up again. I should have been doing more studying and more meditating.

I don't teach on behalf of the institute any longer, therefore, in a way, I lost the backing of that big organization. However, I also understand that had they ever *really* had my back, they would have taught me Yoga from the good books, they would have acted like the gurus they propped themselves up to be and taught me something important. Not diving into those books wasted my time back then and drove my body beyond the healthy point of utilizing asana.

Even though I made some efforts and the desire was always there, I myself avoided the real study of the books because I was intimidated. Luckily I located a teacher/yogi whose life is devoted to yogic purification with special focus on the above mentioned books, who has helped me understand.

So for the last four years, when someone random asks me this seemingly simply answered question of what kind of yoga I teach, I have been drawing what probably looks to the listener like a blank.

However, within me, what is happening is certainly not a blank. I am internally reviewing the words just asked of me and making an analysis of just how much this person actually even knows about the very question they ask.

The asker thinks she's helping me out and offers some options, as I am still not answering: "Do you teach Flow Yoga? Vinyasa? Kundalini? Hatha?"

I hear myself explaining that I teach the original yoga from the scriptural texts. She looks annoyed and says she doesn't know what that is. I say I teach from the Yoga Sutras and Bhagavad Gita, I don't even get to mention the Pradipika before I realize I'm just pissing her off more.

I know what she wants so I cave and say I teach Kundalini Yoga - which is true, but essentially meaningless to her. Her question made it clear she doesn't understand the words she was using.

Imagine you were going to ask a person about a Catechism class they taught but you knew little about it and barely spoke the language you were using. It might sound as smart as this: "What type of Catholicism do you teach? Do you teach Christian Catholicism? Religious Catholicism? Theological Catholicism? "

As you can see through the use of the English, these words have very similar meanings and the follow up questions don't make much sense.

I sometimes feel lost in a world of yoga where no one wants to talk about yoga. No one seems to know or care just how profoundly important Yoga is. Rather I see a strange, stubborn insistence on misrepresenting it - a digging in of the heels and hostile reactions to real information. Yoga redefinition teachers like Rodney Yee, Shiva Rea, Seane Corne and Somebody Stiles who run around the world glorifying themselves at the expense of accurate yoga truth are, in my book, committing a misdeed of unimaginable consequence.

I remember when Oprah started showing interest in Yoga, back in the early 2000's. It made me nervous due to her status as reigning queen of new-age-ification. Then Madonna showed interest in yoga and it became even more mainstream popular. I thought to myself at the time that Madonna would never be the same once she learned about yoga. Obviously, she didn't change and her interest, at least publically, did not venture beyond exploiting postures. Soon after she starred in a movie featuring her as a yoga teacher, she came out with even more superficial music material.

As a Yogini, these things scared me and made me realize that there was a possibility that due to this public misrepresentation of Yoga, I might not be taken seriously.

I write this article because after all this time of having Yoga in the west, look at where it is. Celebrity yoga teachers are basically the bottom of the barrel and that includes those of Eastern descent (i.e. Bikram). I do not excuse someone from misinforming the public due to nationality or a pleasing accent.

It's up to us who call ourselves teachers to actually teach. But to teach you have to learn and the books are right there.

Inescapable concepts one should be prepared to hear about in a Yoga class:

- Reincarnation
- Karma/Phalam (action/result)
- Supreme Being(s)
- That there is a difference between the spirit, the subtle body and the physical body.
- That the world will go on as it is without you after you

liberate.

- That our authorities are great yogi masters like Patanjali, Lord Krishna, Lord Shiva and Swatmarama.
- That we can liberate ourselves through this precise, perfected program on detachment.

If any of the above offends you and yet you say are into Yoga, it might be a good idea to take a second look at what you are doing.

25
The Buying and Selling of Yoga
3 Different Groups of Yoga Users
& a Question for Each

This article addresses 3 categories of 'yoga users' and asks a fundamental question for each to consider. I don't want to offend with use of categorizations, however, sorting things out can help shed light on a matter and help reality come into focus.

I wonder, has yoga changed so much since the historical days of the Mahabharata where we learn of kings, queens, warriors and householders who applied yoga to their life (and after life) endeavors?

Or, is yoga really fodder for a business model to be applied to it?

Daily, ads pop up on my FB newsfeed encouraging me to "Use these tips to make your yoga business BOOM!"? Simply because I have the word yoga in my name, the cultural expectation is for me to take it into business.

Is this ok with us?

Should we continue to accept and encourage the redefining of yoga as it has been so thoroughly in the west and to some extent even in the east?

Yoga is generally treated like a second hand spiritual practice. It is meme'd on, made light of, made fun of and presented by Instagram celebs as the ultimate, sexy, trendy lifestyle of happiness and positivity.

I remember enduring the supermodel Christy Turlington on Oprah, slinging her line of 'yoga' clothes while I struggled with the Sutras, naively waiting during the program for Oprah to bring something up of relevance to the scriptural context of Yoga.

I stomached, and maybe you did too, Madonna's yoga phase in which she used contortionism to bring attention to herself and her new movie– while I made trip after trip to book stores in search of the best translation of the Bhagavad Gita and doing side by side comparisons.

I fought off a rising heart rate when, time after time, some city dwelling entrepreneur/yoga celebrity wannabe made a big dollar deal on the back of this ancient mystic practice of spiritual transmigration, launching yet another charlatan into superstardom.

What is Yoga?

One of the biggest problems I observe is that yoga is deceptively marketed as non-religious, when it is actually very religious, the most religious, albeit of the isolationist sort, but religious, by definition, nonetheless. Yoga's objectives are 100% spiritually inclined and Deity oriented yet it isn't protected with reverence or respect the way other religions are, is it?

Have you ever seen Christianity marketed for arthritis?

How about Judaism for diabetes?

Or Hinduism for stress relief?

The fight for yoga to be used in public schools demonstrates the lack of knowledge society has for this to even be a question. Pick up one traditional yoga scripture and discover that the God(s) is there from beginning to end and the whole point of taking on yoga is ultimate togetherness with God. Wrong or right, this requires it fall under our civic principle of separation of church and state.

In its completeness yoga contains within in it an exercise expectation for physical and subtle body purification purposes. These exercises are traditionally done privately, relatively quietly, alone, outside and with supreme focus and devotion.

Yet here we are today. Americans, especially females, took to the aesthetic beauty of the postures and the exploitation we witness today began and continues to gather momentum. Many celebrity teachers are perfect examples of the wild exploitation of yoga asana as a means toward epidemic exhibitionism.

Sorting It Out

As I said before, it may not be popular to put things in categories but I find it useful considering the current situation at hand. Application of yoga, meaning restraint or detachment, helps us clear our minds, systematize our lives, de-emotionalize and break things down so that we have a fighting chance at seeing the forest through the trees.

To do this we have to pull some things apart to get a better look.

Things like: Who are the main groups in the world using what they call yoga and what are they using it for?

Here goes.

The Three Groups

The first group is Mainstream yoga, the biggest group. Presented by yoga celebrities, business owners, conference organizers, festival gatherers, studio owners and yoga teachers attempting to make a living off teaching 'yoga'. In simple economic terms they are the money changers of the yoga-business world. They vie for opportunity to make deals with even bigger money changers. This group includes anyone who applies a business model to yoga. They almost always tell a story of trauma, depression or injury that led them to practice the stretching and relaxing techniques they call yoga. This group includes mainstream uninformed yoga students who are the fuel ($) behind the phenomenon.

The full commercialization of Yoga has been brought to fruition by savvy capitalist minds from this group. Consumer driven yoga culture is currently headed up by self-proclaimed peace seeking business moguls calling themselves yogi's while projecting an innocent wish to bring the 'message' of yoga to the masses. Ambassadors, they think of themselves, links between the old and the new yoga.

Through objective observation it does appear that the mainstream message is 99 % focused on physical fitness and trendy lifestyle. They use contortionism and attractive bodies captivating the public to aspire to be (buy) something more. We find that yoga is professionally, convincingly sold by big name, very popular business adventurists who drop just enough Sanskrit and just enough philosophy to convince uniformed others that their message is actually yoga.

An example. One big name currently making waves due to questionable alliances and business practices is a person called Kino MacGregor, a teacher who behaves in ways forbidden by the guru she claims devotion. Embroiled with other money changers in an ugly battle over ethics, money, contracts, lawsuits, Kino captivates her devotees with her gymnastic poses she more than generously shares everywhere. To hear anything she might say regarding a relevant text like the Yoga Sutras, beyond verse one, you will pay a monthly subscription to her membership organization which capitalizes on all things sacred.

2. The second group of yoga users is yogically interested Indians.

Indians who possess at least some affection for yoga are understandably upset by the disturbing explosion of misinformation surrounding this sacred application - an application that, in their history, has been regarded as the most supreme of spiritual practices.

Yoga was given by the Gods and sages to the ancestors of modern Indians and it is in their preserved ancient texts that we find out what yoga is.

However, we have to remember that it was Indians themselves who brought the message of yoga to the shores of the west. We are familiar with names like Yogananda, Vivekananda and Vishnu-devananda. Each had their own sects to represent and essentially sold yoga in some modified format to the American public. A format palatable to the western attitude and one which often stretched or warped the truth of yoga's most important goals and practices. Big money was and still is involved.

I was told numerous times while receiving training at the Sivananda Yoga Academy that yogic Hindu's built ashrams in America because souls from the east were reincarnating in the west and needed their yoga! In practice though, I haven't experienced this to be the actual mindset.

Since I was born into a white body in the west, some, especially caste conscious Indians possessive of or protective of information, may see me as an impostor, an appropriator, a 'self-declared' yogini - rather than in the light of reincarnation, evolution and self-development.

The Indian factor in yoga is a most complex subject due to the caste structure limitations and varying levels of belief in and understanding of reincarnation. I've personally had Indian yoga students (every single one a doctor) show up to class who were the most humble and gracious students ever, openly admitting to knowing literally nothing about yoga. I've been invited into the home of a student, an Indian single father, to speak to his sons on yoga because he knew nothing to tell them about it - but wanted them to hear of their ancestor's ancient past and the glories of the yoga.

3. The third group of yoga users are genuine devotees of the true practice of yoga and its promise of transmigration to the spiritual world to be with God, Ishwara.

This group are souls who are yoga dependents. If yoga were considered a deity, they would be devotees.

They are the only group that, in my opinion, should even consider teaching.

They are driven for yoga for more than injury recovery, healthcare, relaxation or a hobby after a dance career. These are the souls who pursue the yoga and to who's mind a business deal would never even cross.

These students have their nose in the books:

- The Bhagavad Gita
- The Yoga Sutras
- The Hatha Yoga Pradipika.

Their little cannon of holy books.

Their curiosity regarding the depth of these psychological wonders is nearly insatiable.

Their lives revolve around them just the way a good Christian can always refer to a verse in the bible during any life circumstance.

Three Questions, One for Each Group

The question for the first group, Mainstreamers, is this:

✓ If you stop making a business of yoga, even stop teaching yoga as you traditionally do, what would happen to your own studies and practice if you were on your own with no devotees, no special attention, no pics, no Instagram, no recognition? If you could tell no one you do yoga for the rest of your life would you still do it?

The question for the second group (Indians) is:

✓ What do you really believe (or know) about reincarnation? If you really believe that souls reincarnate (and we find ample evidence of this in Vedic texts) then why is race and geography playing such a role in the upset over Yoga in the west?

Do you really believe that I could be a yogini who has incarnated into bodies of other races in other parts of the world only to end up in the body I use to write this article today?

(Depending on how Indians answer this determines how our cultures can proceed forth productively. If Indians see westerns as their own ancestors, ancestors in need of deep spiritual options just as they are, than I think hand and hand, this could be a potentially easy fix. But knowledge of reincarnation is imperative.)

The question for the third group (Devotees) is:

- ✓ What's your role in this, if any? You are lucky if you have no part to play in this and unlike myself, have no words compelled to come out of your mouth about it. So if you ask yourself this question and find no energy within your psyche to participate in being critical toward it, count yourself as lucky.

In Conclusion, Some Recommendations:

If you are making a business on yoga maybe shut it down. There is really good reason to this for yourself and others. Take the business out of Yoga and apply the Yoga to the business of your life.

Whether you are a nurse, a farmer, an engineer, hairdresser, banker, cop, whatever your skill, yoga is meant to be applied to it.

Application of Yoga is a full time job

If you apply yoga to your life you might find it takes up a lot of your focus. It takes effort and sacrifice. Its demands on adherence to lifestyle regulation consumes a lot of your energy…and for the true devotee, this is a welcome condition.

I think it's time to tame the beast that has become this misapplication of the ultimate application.

I suggest a boycott of consumerist yoga.

And no more using the word out of context.

Demand that your teacher know things, relevant things, advanced things.

Ask questions in class.

No more adoration of the Emperor who wore no clothes.

Let us, this generation of yoga practitioners, care enough about the future of yoga to bring this exploitation to an end.

26

Is it a Stretch Class? Or is it Yoga How to Tell the Difference

I myself was teaching yoga before I had any business doing so. Society told me I could though. There were no laws or regulations against me saying I was a yoga teacher and no assessor came around to check on my classes or question my knowledge.

Even a respected institute of yoga, the Sivananda Yoga Vedanta School, gave me a paper certificate with a fancy Sanskrit title and ordained me to teach yoga. It only took $1500, one month of following the ashram rules and passing an exam and I was a teacher of what?

It's no big deal though, right? It's just yoga, right?

It is a big deal that myself and millions of people in the world are considered certified teachers of the MOST COMPLEX AND HIGHLY PSYCHOLOGICAL FORM OF SELF ACCOUNTABILITY AND PURIFICATION SYSTEM EVER STANDARDIZED BY MAN THROUGH HIS RELATIONSHIP WITH SUPERNATURAL BEINGS -. A SYSTEM OF LIFESTYLE REGULATION AND MEDITATION SO INTRICATE, COMPLICATED AND ULTIMATELY LIBERATING THAT OUR OWN SCRIPTURES DEEM IT APPROPRIATE FOR FEW BEINGS.

Here, as a person who has made mistakes in the past and learned from them, I offer a list of what makes a yoga class a yoga class and what makes a stretch class a stretch class.

What makes it Yoga?

It's religious. Boom. Most teachers won't admit it to their classes and some don't even know it. The religiosity of yoga cannot be extracted from the goals because they rely on each other. Marketing something as religious puts limits on the potential for paying customers since most people come to yoga for physical and mental health related reasons – not because they are interested in spiritual liberation through the instruction of Lord Shiva or Lord Krishna or Patanjali. Studios need more, not less students - because of money. So they leave the deities out of the teachings, which just as with Christianity or any religion, nullifies the goal of the practice.

(If yoga teachers would honestly push for legislation to make yoga studios religious centers, they could become tax exempt, couldn't they?)

The primary scriptures are what the teacher focuses on. Even during exercises. The Yoga Sutras and Pradipika are gold for teaching material yet if you find that the teacher isn't especially focused on teaching the substance in them, you'd be wise to become suspicious that she's making up what she thinks Yoga is, or wants it to be, combined with what she's been told by mainstream culture and new age books on the subject.

No music. This one isn't popular. Personally I had way more students when I was a two-bit-new-age-happy-little-know-nothing teacher offering 'themed' classes which included music. I even did a class to the tunes of Led Zeppelin back in the day. (major face palm)

Music has its place in our lives and in the execution of conscious living. However, when it comes to practicing yoga, Patanjali requires elimination of distraction. Music stirs emotion and that's not what we're doing. We are instructed to purify and take control of the tendency of emotional and mental fluctuations. Yoga requires proper focus on lifestyle, postures, breathing, mystic exercises, internalized focus, lack of emotion, lack of memory, lack of imagination, deep concentration and completion of insight. We don't let ourselves be dependent on music to get us into a certain mood for yoga. The yoga itself will shift you in the correct mood but it takes effort. It's that effort that empowers us.

As a former kirtan band leader I say this with due respect to the honored practice of devotional chanting. But as my own practice progressed, I left behind the activity of group chanting. Eventually I admitted to myself it was barren of authenticity.

Yoga postures are performed so that the subtle body can be moved into certain positions for optimum cleaning access. Subtle body anatomy is the focus in class, not physical. Yoga teachers aren't physical therapists or physical anatomy experts. Indeed, they should strive always to be subtle, or psychological body anatomy experts. If any graphics of the body are used in class they should most often be of the subtle system not the physical. In a genuine yoga class the teacher is regularly redirecting the students focus onto the subtle body.

Meditation, purely yogic, according to Patanjali, is required after the asana/pranayama/pratyahara. Meditation is the main point of performing the postures with breathing which serve to prepare the mental space for quietude and high vibrancy during meditation. Meditation is performed immediately after the exercises and is done in silence so that naad sound can be accessed and meditated upon. (Again about the music – it inhibits proper naad listening, it does not enhance it. The only instrument helpful is a singing bowl or chime, used momentarily only to induce the awareness of naad at the beginning of the mediation.)

What makes it a stretch class?

None or little of the above occurs.

Physical stretching and its health benefits are the focus.

You hear words like Namaste, Om, Om Namah Sivaya, Jai Ma and the like. You'll likely hear Sanskrit names of postures. In fact you may hear them ad naseum (i.e. chaturanga).

It's usually new agey and self-helpy. A lot of 'yoga' teachers are more like self-help-stretch teachers. Readings, that have little or nothing to do with the goals of yoga found in our scriptures, are favored, and often quite popular.

A lot of physical adjustments made by the teacher. This is an unconscious smoke and mirrors trick that makes the teacher seem knowledgeable as a 'Yoga' teacher. This illusion depends on the ignorance of the students because most people think yoga means postures. And if the teacher knows the postures so well, she must understand yoga, right?

The teacher tells you that there are many kinds of yoga, then says some Sanskrit words and names – such as vinyasa, ashtanga, kundalini, Iyengar, Sivananda.....but fails to explain that any form of postural yoga falls under the domain of Hatha yoga who's instruction is found in our authority text the Hatha Yoga Pradipika. This error is so prevalent it is made regularly by some of the so called highest authorities on yoga in the mainstream.

That's my list.

We have the documents explaining this magnificent Yoga, we have information from the gods of Yoga themselves for the highest inspiration and yet, most Yoga classes are just glorified stretch classes. I hope this changes and I hope my lists, cheeky as they may be, might help.

27
The Exploitation of Yoga Asana

It's everywhere. I used to do it. There I am pictured above doing it. You may be doing it too - exploiting the asana.

You know what I'm talking about. Using pictures of yourself in asana to draw students or simply impress others.

How often do you find yourself taking pictures here and there, in front of this or that, in an asana?

How often to you advertise and teach yoga as an exercise class resulting in better physical health and relaxation?

Ask yourself these questions:

Do I identify Yoga primarily with physical postures?

Do I feel a need to constantly identify myself with asana?

Do asana provide me with an identity that I like?

Do I sexualize asana.....and pretend I don't?

Do I use asana as a fashion statement?

Do I, if I am a teacher, avoid lecturing to my class about actual Yoga doctrine?

Do I see teaching asana as a way to make money?

~~~~~~~

The temptation is real. These Instagram and YouTube yoga celebs are serious business about the exploitation of yoga into the ultimate sexy, trendy, life$tyle life$tyle.

And despite my own personal true love for Yoga's original eight limbs, I once did *some* of these things too.

(*Some*, I say, I didn't lose my mind. I can look back on my life and know that I *never* once called myself a magical unicorn aerial rainbow yoga goddess. I would never have considered taking the exploitation to such extremes.)

Asana, without the other limbs of yoga is nothing but stretching and goes nowhere in terms of Yoga goals and is as ordinary as any other exercise. As a 'yoga' teacher myself I could no longer stand to be what I actually was - *an expert stretch and relaxation instructor* who, at the end of a peaceful class read something nice from Vivekananda or Deepak Chopra, bowed and said Namaste – oh and took plenty of pictures of postures. The fancier, the better.

How the hell was I a yoga teacher when, at that time, I wouldn't have been able to give a clear, contextual lecture on the subject?

In front of Hindu scholars?

Back then, just because I could perform advanced physical stretches our society labels as 'Yoga', did *not* make me a Yoga teacher.

Back then, just because I attended a 'respected' teacher training and was given a meaningless, unregulated certification, also did *not* make me a yoga teacher.

Sure I was a stretch expert with a soothing voice, philosophical thoughts and easily parroted, watered-down yoga philosophy, but was I really a Yoga teacher?

Are you?

During those long years of teaching I craved a deeper understanding, insight and context for yoga.

I longed for real knowledge of the Bhagavad Gita, the Yoga Sutras and the Hatha Yoga Pradipika but couldn't seem to find a translation or commentary that offered me the penetrating insight I knew must exist somewhere in this world.

I searched and searched, read and read, kept practicing and one day, I found it - and it changed everything.

I finally found it by finding the right translations of the Yoga Sutras, Bhagavad Gita and the Pradipika.

(Translations of these texts are not all equal, many are vague and wishy-washy. Some are mediocre and some are straight up manipulative in translation.)

A translation of anything depends completely on the translators grasp on BOTH languages.

Not just a grasp on one and partially of the other - resulting in half assed translations, resulting in half assed commentaries, resulting in half assed understanding by readers.

What I found in the translations and commentaries by a mahayogi named Michael Beloved lifted my mind into an exalted new understanding. His handle of both languages is beyond anything I had hoped for and combined with his comprehension, stunning insight and instruction on application of yoga is a gift to those seeking understanding of this practice.

My point is I would love for Yoga to be taken seriously. As it stands now, it is not. Its meme'd, made fun of, made light of and being forced as a non-spiritual exercise into the public school system. Of course stretching and relaxation should be taught to everyone, but yoga is something super mystical, totally spiritual, and completely focused on scriptural and philosophical study making it inappropriate for a civic system which imposes separation of church and state.

It's not always easy to be a devotee of something so religious in nature and yet falsely labeled as non-religious. It gives people a lot of room to disrespect it.

It's not always easy to be a devotee of a practice so focused on leaving this world while mainstream yoga culture incessantly markets it as a fitness lifestyle for social activist types who want to see world peace in a place that has never known anything of the sort.

When, in fact, Yoga is a very selfish enterprise, totally focused on the liberation of the individual and his/her escape from this traumatic dimension.

An example. The ahimsa portion of the yamas is routinely exploited by social activist style yoga teachers who put pressure on society to recognize it. Yet it's not meant for them, it's meant for someone ready to leave clear up his/her karmas and transcend this level of existence. In the context of Yoga though, this lack of violent behavior is curbed by the individual yogin not necessarily to change the world, but to purify just him/herself for the purposes of insight and transcendence. When we study the richness of the *Bhagavad Gita*, we learn from Lord Krishna that we are not expected to solve what we perceive as the problems of this world but rather, to figure our own individual way out of it through knowledge of the righteous duties we must perform to pay off our karmic debt and be released from spiritual incarceration.

This is yoga instruction.

Bottom Line

Yoga is so special, so unique in this strange creation. It deserves to be understood that the exercise portion of Yoga is necessary but done privately and purposefully for spiritual ambitions, not social accolades. Deities and yoga masters are astrally present as a true yogi or yogini practices the steps of yoga and the acknowledgement of our efforts are recorded and observed by them, not by our fellow Earthlings, as it is not with them that we aspire to be.

I would love for you to have a reason to move beyond the asana exploitation and your presentation of it as 'Yoga'.

I would love to see Yoga teachers either bring their philosophical teachings on the Yoga scriptures out from behind their backs and start teaching them as primary Yoga, or start learning Yoga philosophy in the first place and teach it along with the rest of the limbs.

I would love it if a Yoga class only sometimes included asana because yoga students already have a strong *home practice* and don't juvenilely rely on a teacher for this portion of their practice. They rely on the teacher for it to only some extent, but to a far greater extent the reliance is on the philosophical wisdom of the teacher. This is what makes a Yoga teacher a Yoga teacher.

To experience my own Yoga class in a book form please see my book: Kundalini Yoga Home Practice by devaPriya Yogini.

If we ask ourselves questions about our practice, maybe we will have a better idea as to what our real motivations in Yoga are.

Then, if we truly love the Yoga, its holy texts and its requirements, then maybe you, like me, can get to work and stop exploiting Yoga asana.

Portion on Kundalini

28
All Hatha Yoga IS Kundalini Yoga

All Hatha Yoga is Kundalini Yoga ......but you may have to be actively raising kundalini daily to understand why.

There is so much ambiguity regarding the Sanskrit words. Most of the time the person using the word is using it how they've been told to use it rather than how they have individually learned, experienced and studied how to use it. Fortunately, we all have the option of second guessing vague things we have accepted in the past - to seek out better, fuller answers.

First of all, hatha yoga is never just asana, much less just certain asana or a certain method of asana.

We find out what Hatha Yoga is from The Hatha Yoga Pradipika, recorded by the yogi Swatmarama and not from anywhere else. Whatever we hear from anyone regarding hatha yoga must be verified by putting it up against what we read in the text. Otherwise, we are just making it up.

These are the six limbs of Hatha Yoga:

1. Mystic Exercises (Asana)
2. Breath Infusion (Pranayama)
3. Retraction of Attention (Pratyahara)
4. Effortful focus (Dharana)
5. Spontaneous meditation (Dhyana)
6. Complete Insight (Samadhi)

Note that these are the six highest limbs of Patanjali's eight limbs. The first two limbs, yamas and niyamas are not included in Swatmarama's Hatha Yoga because the student using this instruction will be moved away from society and large and will no longer have a need to curb his/her social dealing.

Since this article is about how Hatha Yoga *is* Kundalini Yoga, I will begin by *defining* the words. Sanskrit words are not just words; each word is more like an entire file - one that is not always easy to open. Most explanations on Sanskrit words in Yoga culture, even those offered by high caste Indians, are mostly vague and redundant. Personally, I won't remain stuck with depthless hit or miss explanations on Yoga I've been given in the past from very reputable institutions and swamis. And even though I am not into whimsical discussions that lack proper textual mention, if you genuinely feel my definitions are inaccurate, please cite the referential evidence from the Hatha Yoga Pradipika.

Here are the definitions - then I will continue my point.

Hatha: *Literal translation, 'sun moon'. Understood as, 'manipulation' and also 'something difficult to do'.* On the most practical level of our yoga practice, hatha means 'manipulation'. All 6 steps Swatmarama identifies are considered *manipulations*. During yogic exercises the body, mind, breathing and attention are manipulated for the purposes of psychological clean out. Energy channels, physical and psychic organs and the many tubes and pumps that circulate the energy of this universal system through the psyche are cleaned. Each mind is a psychic machine operated by natural forces, hatha yoga is the method by which the passenger (atma) or core-self, becomes aware of itself and takes conscious control of the vehicle by applying a disciplined process of purification for spiritual (self/atma) liberation. Remember, the 3 highest stages, dharana, dhyana, and samadhi are also included in this Hatha Yoga as they are the manipulation of the attention energies to higher concentration forces, leading to the acquisition of complete insight and the beginnings of spiritual life, the goal of the practice.

Yoga: *Literal translation, 'yoke' or 'restraint'.* A system of austerity for self-purification and ultimate liberation from material creation/samsara. Holy source texts include: *The Bhagavad Gita, Patanjali Yoga Sutras* and the *Hatha Yoga Pradipika*. We find the standardization of yoga in the *Yoga Sutras* in which Patanjali explains the 8 fold (ashtanga) process. Without this text yoga would remain extremely mysterious and difficult to collect much less grasp. Bhagavad Gita gives us the philosophical/spiritual/deeply theological knowledge and the Pradipika gives us the practical/ instructional/kriya knowledge. These 3 texts embody the canon of Yoga instruction.

Kundalini: *Literal translation, 'coiled she-serpent'.* In the body and mind it is running everything. It runs the whole universe too. It is the electrical box of your psyche (psychological house) located in the geographic center of the subtle body near the base of the spine close to the reproductive organs. The epicenter of instinct and all mental-physical functions, it is the energy vortex where the mind does its most potent work throughout intricate bodily and psychological functions

Kundalini energy is NOT spiritual energy - it is psychological and elemental energy, shifty and evolving. It is a separate entity from spiritual energy. Within the kundalini life force, inside the subtle body container, living up in the head space is the spiritual person, the atma, or core-self.

So why do I say that all hatha (manipulation) Yoga is kundalini Yoga? Why do I say that essentially *all* serious yogic exercise should be understood as kundalini yoga?

Because *kundalini* is the *target* of all *Hatha* Yoga practice.

The cleaning AND the transcendental raising of the kundalini light force from the base of the body into the head of the body.

This is an experience like no other and is special to Yoga, and is the sole purpose of mystic asana and pranayama.

Yoga targets nature. The kundalini life force intelligence within the individual body is that nature. The Yoga process acts to reform the nature suit you keep being born into, subjected to, through continuous cycles of birth and death. As yogins, we find this traumatic and desire existence in a spiritual realm. We take seriously our hatha yoga practice to get us there.

We manipulate it so that we can manipulate the mind into a condition ripe for meditation wherein the core-self can sit alone with itself, with naad sound and with higher concentration sources and forces. These are the higher stages and experiences of Yogic meditation.

The concentration of kundalini life force in the base of the spine is a form of light. As the asana and pranayama open things up and release energies, that light becomes cleaner, brighter, movable and willing, for the moment, to move out of its primary residence in the groin. By physical and subtle internal manipulations, locks (bandhas), we are able to guide kundalini light through the central spine and into the head, where the self experiences a transcendental state of consciousness known as a kundalini rise.

It is about taking control of the electrical box in the body you live in, instead of it controlling you.

Hatha Yoga is about mastering the habits and tendencies of that electrical box and the whole system it operates. A yogin is an electrician of sorts.

It requires a lot of study, practice and introspection. Electrical systems can be intimidating and tricky. Elexctricity demands respect and true understanding of how electricity really works is often know only to the professionals due to the complexities and dangers. Those practicing kundalini Yoga become professional subtle body electricians.

Yoga is about restraining the kundalini and then mastering its potential, something it can never do on its own - exclusively for the purpose of spiritual freedom from the whole thing.

This material creation is not the only world.

The spiritual world exists too and yoga shows us how to make our best attempt to achieve it.

In terms of yoga, our ability to perform this manipulation is the whole point of bothering to evolve into a human form to begin with.

This level of control mastery is quite exclusive to Yoga. I've not found this echelon of command over the self in any other single disciple.

Bottom Line

Gymnastic Yoga is not Yoga. It doesn't matter what Swami's name is attached to it or how many worshipful followers he has. It's gymnastics, calisthenics. If someone offers hatha Yoga in a list of a bunch of other 'types' of Yoga, you will know that they don't understand the words they are using.

All these Yogas;

Iyengar, Vinyasa, Bikram, Yin, Sivananda, Ashtanga, restorative - add any name or word to the list….if they are not incorporating the asana with the pranayama with the pratyahara with the 3 highest meditation stages of insight, it is NOT Yoga and you should not allow yourself to be short changed:

Don't be cheated or cheat yourself.

Yoga is when you are following Gita, Sutras and Pradipika.

It is 8 steps if you are still living in the society.

It is 6 steps if you are not.

Either way, there you are.

Get to the kundalini, study it, clean it with aggressive breathing, internalize all your attention, and then sit to meditate without allowing the mind to be active.

Read the Kundalini Hatha Yoga Pradipika translation and commentary by Michael Beloved!

Then you have guaranteed found HathaYoga.

29

If You're Not Raising Kundalini Causing Transcendental Events, Are You Really Practicing Yoga?

Rarely does a Yoga student learn and apply the secret to a real yogic exercise practice. Most students accept what they're offered at a Yoga studio by a certified 'teacher' as being yoga but the truth is that very few people, even well-meaning teachers, understand what it really means to perform Yoga exercises.

It was only 6 years ago that I came to understand that despite a dedicated 15 years of practice and teaching, I was not really practicing, or teaching, Yoga.

Why?

- ✓ I wasn't harnessing and raising kundalini. I wasn't pushing my students to do so either, I didn't know I should be and I didn't know how.
- ✓ I wasn't having controlled transcendental events during my practice nor were students.
- ✓ I wasn't using the locks (bandhas) properly.
- ✓ I wasn't using breath infusion aggressively enough to really prepare my body and psyche for the transcendental event of kundalini raising and meditation.
- ✓ I wasn't studying proper translations of the Yoga Source Texts to even comprehend what Yoga's goals were.

The secret seems to be that, news flash, *transcendental events are supposed to be part and parcel of a Yoga exercise practice*. If you're not having them, yet say you are practicing 'Yoga', then at least you should be actively working toward them.

Your Yoga 'teacher' should be assisting you greatly in moving toward them.

In fact, your teacher will be the person literally holding up the weight of your body as you fall unconscious the first few times you raise kundalini into your head. She will be the one embracing your possessed body and whispering in your ear to 'pull in the mind lock!' and to 'pull in your chin lock!' as your eyelids involuntarily flutter, your eyeballs roll up toward your third eye, and your facial muscles twitch and dance as kundalini moves through channels of your body that may have never been touched by such grace energy.

She may even wipe tears from your cheeks as you return to your body with all the emotion of having had experienced something beyond yourself, something psychedelic, something transcendental.

She will be your protector until you are able to successfully apply the internal locking mechanisms, bandhas, which enable you to align your spine and subtle body in such a way that you remain conscious in your body, witnessing, as kundalini life force energy moves up into your head and you experience another dimension of light, color, shape, sound, combined with feelings of bliss and transcenent joy.

This all happens during exercises (asana) and breath infusion (pranayama)!

This is what real Yogi's are doing and this is what Yoga teachers should be doing.

Why?

Because this is what prepares us to sit down and practice yogic style meditation, the point of all this effort! The highest three limbs of the 8 fold path Patanjali standardized for us!

And Yogic meditation isn't meant to have you stay in the here and now forever watching your breath and being mindful, no! Yogic meditation means for you to *detach* yourself from normal mental activities and *attach* yourself to naad sound, the inner Om, riding it like a cosmic conveyor belt to ever higher awareness's.

As "Yoga" practitioners we should really ask ourselves about our own exercise practice.

Why am I doing these asana?

Why do I stretch my body and breathe it with special exercises and call it Yoga, a word not from my own language? (This can include Indian's as most Indian's do not speak or study Sanskrit.)

What is my goal in doing these exercises and are my goals the same as those itemized in the source texts which expound this ancient, foreign concept, Yoga?

If my honest answer is that I am stretching for reasons like wellness, relaxation, peace of mind and long life, yet I have little desire to understand "Yoga", one of the six astika (meaning the belief in the self) schools of Hinduism, then I might consider reevaluating my use of the word.

Beyond even my training at the renowned Sivananda ashram teacher program, I spent years reading about Yoga from every Tom, Dick and Harry guru with 'ananda' at the end of his name. My heart was in the right place and I was certainly staying physically and mentally healthy. But I was not making progress in terms of understanding the truly transcendental effects I knew Yoga promised in those scriptures.

Beginning in 2013 I had the good luck to study academic translations and commentaries of the Hatha Yoga Pradipika, Yoga

Sutras and Bhagavad Gita and to study under their author, a non-institutional, no nonsense kundalini master, Michael Beloved.

I was forced to accept what I had suspected; that I had barely scratched the surface of what I thought a Yoga practice was. Michael's insights make even the most revered guru philosophers look like children - and I certainly don't say this to belittle them, it is simply true. His mystic skills, understanding of reincarnation, translations and purports of the Yogic scriptures, humility, and his personal daily practice are unparalleled. His grasp and application of Yoga is something I never imagined being lucky enough to find in this world, yet here it exists. And every day my practice deepens, my understanding expands, due to association with him.

Again I say, we should all question ourselves about our own so called Yoga practice. It's worth it and causes us to know ourselves, our intentions and our goals so much better.

It also saves Yoga from further denigration.

So please stretch and hyperventilate yourself into controlled mystic events. Events that happen directly to you, not just stuff you've read about.

Look around you, you can't see it, but the most powerful chemical drug surrounds you, waits for you to make use of it for transcendence. Air. O2. Nothing is more powerful to your genuine kundalini practice than the use you can make of air.

The Question of Raising Kundalini

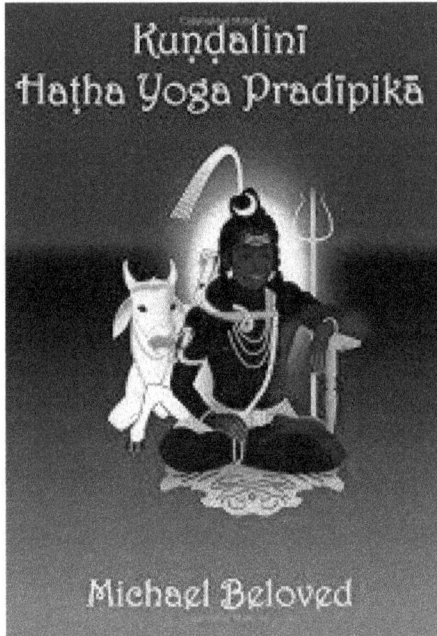

Kundalini is already active in our body and mind, it does not need 'activation', it is not dormant. It is already in charge of all the functions of the physical and the subtle body and can be found everywhere within them. You can feel it right now, beating your heart and digesting your last meal.

Kundalini gets the body/mind up in the morning and puts it down at night. It makes the body hungry, horny, excited, sad, clingy, nostalgic, goal oriented, depressed. It is and does everything you have ever experienced in this universe.

There is an epicenter, or, concentrated portion, of kundalini located at the base of the spine, in the lower chakras, very close to the genital organs, under the bulky digestive system. Most of kundalini's daily functions have to do with survival behaviors such as eating, sleeping, reproducing and reacting. Occasionally the kundalini will feel and do other things slightly out of the ordinary in reactivity to something. It may produce strong emotions that it regards as special. Emotions such as; elation from singing with the congregation at church, or deep feelings, goosebumps and general ASMR, from chanting mantras, joy from dancing, connection through praying or even peace while meditating.

Even though kundalini life force is already active within each of us, even the animals, we should not be foolish enough to conclude that because of a mantra or the touch of a guru that it will spontaneously rise up within the body, spread its self out blissfully and cause a person to be suddenly enlightened and with upgraded DNA.

It's a fancy thought but not the way it works. Most events that people describe as 'kundalini activations' are actually 99% normal, mundane, high end emotional experiences of the nervous system and have little to do with Hatha Yoga manipulations of kundalini – that is, if we are really into Yoga and not an imposter practice.

If you are into Yoga, your interest in kundalini is different than the average persons. The average person doesn't even fathom what kundalini is or what their spiritual relationship with it might be. In fact they think they are the kundalini. They do not spiritually sort themselves out from it. It is their only known identity.

In Sanskrit this level of consciousness is called "advaita". People at this stage are able to sense out the collective energies of the universe but are not yet able to distinguish themselves within that sea of everything-ness. Nature is adept at keeping us trapped in the stage of non-duality for a long time. She tricks us into thinking we've got it all figured out.

In modern terms it is the 'oneness movement' found in new-age religions.

If you are into genuine yoga your interest in the kundalini life force is in locating it, sensing it out, investigating it, cleaning it, reforming its stubborn, redundant ways, infusing it with oxygen and MANIPULATING (hatha) it with internal physical and psychic maneuvers in order to route its power upward through the body/mind into higher parts of the psyche where its light has the potential to cause a transcendental event and the development of insight. This is the path toward the goal of yoga called samadhi, meaning complete insight. Manipulation of the kundalini is the way.

Done often and over time, these yogically induced events may assist the core self in its venture toward freedom from the very life force it is manipulating.

It's kind of like when Bruce Lee would use the power of his opponent to empower himself.

We manipulate the kundalini life force as empowerment for the spiritual person who is held captive by the whole thing.

Imagine a prisoner in a dark penitentiary who figures out how to temporarily turn all the prison lights on- and everyday he goes and does it again and again, even if the warden (kundalini) is reluctant for him to do so. During those moments when the prison is brightly lit up, the prisoner gets a good look around and with repeated looks, he may begin to figure his way out. Insight develops. With stunning clarity he looks down and all around the prison. He even looks deeply inward, even bringing the light within him, finding himself in another world, which under normal consciousness is undetectable to him.

The light causes him to be able to see and feel things he could not access before.

So if he knows how to do this, should he not go turn on the lights every day?

Or should he become passive, sit and chant, and wait for the light to spontaneously turn on? Why?

If you think kundalini should spontaneously rise and you claim this is what makes you a yogi, than what is the use of our Yoga scriptures?

Where does it even say that in the Pradipika? Or the Gita? Or the Sutras.

On the contrary, our yoga books let us know in no uncertain terms that yoga takes effort, will power and determination. It takes work. It is work.

Please do not let anyone tell you that this is not to be done every day. It is to be done every day. It is safe when done right. It is safe when we understand breath infusion and the locks. Don't forfeit your potential to daily experience a transcendental event, for is a blessing from God. It is our way out. It is the path to the purified state required to reach higher dimensions.

So what is Yogic Kundalini Manipulation?

We use the breath which uses the oxygen which is the highest of Earthly elements yogically speaking. However, there is one more element even higher than the air which is accessed by the air and by the magic of yoga asana, and that is the inner light. We access the inner light, the light of the subtle body, concentrated in the kundalini bulb at the base of the spine and we pull it up over and over again, unfurling it, in order to fill the bodies and provide the self with a well-lit environment – an environment in which nothing, no pollutant, no impurity, no anxiety, can hide out trying to screw up our big liberation plans!!!!!!!!

I was practicing and teaching yoga for nearly 15 years before I learned I was doing it wrong.

I only realized that I had been taught incorrectly, when I was taught correctly.

To finally understand yoga, my greatest desire, the spiritual relief is hard to describe.

Here's the Key:

When I was finally taught by yoga teacher Michael Beloved to perform breath infusion (bhastrika/bellows breathing) during my stretches, to use the locks (bhandas) to stabilize and route kundalini during breath retention, and to use special instigation postures, I finally experienced a transcendental event; an actual kundalini rise into my head which propelled my awareness into a higher dimension. I was no longer aware of my body. My teacher was right there, holding me up as I left my body that way for the first time. The body attempted to fall to the ground. I could hear him in the distance reminding me to hold my chin lock, pull the anus lock up and keep my mind pulled in. I did so and fought to stay physically lucid - even though I felt so psychically celestial.

As my awareness returned to my body and I was able to hold it up myself, I was able to continue studying the event. It was stunning and I knew in that moment that Yoga was everything I had sensed it was but had never been told or shown. Not by any of the big time teachers I had looked into, not by my Sivananda teacher training, not by Swami anybody. All that had been told to me about yoga up to that point had been mostly non-sense, maybe because they were withholding, or maybe because most yoga people are phonies.

I no longer need my teacher to be right there to catch me because he taught me specifically how to handle the kundalini energy myself. This is what the locks are for!! Specifically for this! To keep you in control of your body, your spine in place, braced, locked, for the proper and safe routing of kundalini up the central channel (shushmna nadi) in order for this event to be experienced and studied. This is the magic of Hatha Yoga.

Since then, I've raised kundalini hundreds of time and god willing I will raise it hundreds of times more before I leave this body.

If you truly wish for a Supreme Abode to be your new address then you will surely not sit around and wait for kundalini to rise within you. Instead, you will take the bull by the horns and do it yourself because you can and because you are ready and because the proper instruction IS available. It is not vague and it is not passive.

Yogis are not lazy or new agey, we do not expect for the God to just come to us because we feel we are that special.

Through yoga we become eligible to go to God.

We make ourselves special enough to be with God by shedding the current system that surrounds us and regurgitates us.

We do this by manipulating the system. That is what hatha yoga is, it is 'manipulation' yoga.

A yogi is like a hacker of the subtle body. He learns how he can go in and manipulate his own system to get what he wants, even if that means ultimate destruction of the program in which he lives.

He knows that there exists an abode appropriate for spiritual life on the other side of this material creation. He knows because he's seen glimpses of it often during his kundalini manipulation events and following meditations.

Raising kundalini during a yoga exercise session can cause profound progress in meditation which is done immediately after exercises.

Put yoga to work for what it's for. Stop making it less than it is. It is not glorified stretching, it is so much more and while you're waiting for and telling others that kundalini should spontaneously arise within you "if you are a real yogi", then you're missing the entire point of Yoga and don't understand the first thing about it.

If you do not believe any of this that I have said, please read a worthy translation and commentary of the Hatha Yoga Pradipika. It is hands down, inarguably our authority on Hatha Yoga. I would highly suggest the one by Michael Beloved titled – Kundalini Hatha Yoga Pradipika, as the translation is accurate and the commentaries are deeply insightful. He also doesn't skip any of the verses – all the other translators unfortunately do.

All Hatha Yoga teachers should be using the Hatha Yoga Pradipika as their main standard for practice. They should be reading to their students from it. I realize that for a long time there was not a translation/commentary present in the world that made much sense, but there is now and it's easy to find online.

And….if we want to more about yoga than Shri Swatmarama reveals in the Hatha Yoga Pradipika, then we study Patanajali's Yoga Sutras and the Bhagavad Gita.

31
What's in a Kundalini Rise?
Are they All Created Equal?

Kundalini is the energy of nature her-self. It is the ever mutating force of material life. It literally means 'coiled she-serpent'. In the Bhagavad Gita, Lord Krishna speaks in detail about this material nature - with special emphasis on its three moods, or gunas.

Kundalini is material intelligence, a complex program of evolving energetic elements of various forms, combinations and refinements. These elements provide, or force upon, the spiritual self (atma) an environment, both physical and mental, to operate within.

Each of us is using a subtle body that possesses a battery charge of life force located at the base of the spine. An orb of concentrated electricity, this kundalini charge supports and carries out all physical and subtle body operations – including thought. It exists causelessly. Without it, the physical body would be slumped over dead.

It is this kundalini concentration that is the target of hatha yoga practice.

Right now, if you take awareness to the base of your spine and focus on this region momentarily, you may sense its potency radiating in nearby organs, its urging power, and its dynamic, primordial essence.

As I recently described in a previous essay, the personal kundalini is similar to the Freudian psychological concept of "Id". Western psychology grasps the presence of a generative energy acting as the psychic-material self, an instinctual force operating the functions of physical/subtle living. In the context of Eastern thought, we further understand that the subtle body is inherently compelled to seek and re-seek new bodies through the natural process of reincarnation.

This is the spell that Yoga is meant to break….and is as difficult as you might imagine.

Kundalini is like a little man down in the body, a temporary self that nonetheless feels very real. This little person living down in the base chakras has a periscope-like extension of vital energy reaching up through the center of the body (shushumna nadi), connecting to the intellect. In Sanskrit the intellect is called the' buddhi' organ. It is located in the frontal portion of the subtle brain. The intellect is of course connected to the eyes, ears, nose, mouth and skin, the sensual receptors of external information.

It makes sense when you study it - that the main source of vital, material energy comes from the area of the genital regions. Peeing, pooping, sexing, orgasming, menstruating, birthing, even hunger, fear and creativity - are directly motivated by the kundalini life force at the base of the spine.

So what about kundalini rises?

In this article I would like to address two kinds.

One is what I will call the 'natural' kundalini rise. This type might also be called, involuntary or instinctual. It happens when our senses and/or emotions are stimulated in a way that produces the event. The event involves a rush of pleasure energy that moves through the body and mind, hairs stand on end and the mind feels a sense of elation. Music can provoke it, asmr, stretching, and sudden movements, emotionally-touching events - it can happen on a roller coaster or when you jump out of a plane.

These are natural, spontaneous ways anyone can experience kundalini expressing through the body pleasurably through pre-programmed routes.

I personally remember having the natural type of kundalini rises as a small child of 3 or 4 years old. It would happen when I would hurt myself ironically, like when skinning a knee which hurt like hell. I would be crying really hard and would end up in a state of suspended animation in which I was holding my breath. For whatever reason, I would find myself passing out of my normal physical environment and into a transcendental state of body and mind. A pleasurable energy would move itself through my psyche. I would be stunned into a silent relaxation that I would soon snap out of and return to normal. My mother describes me crying, holding my breath, turning a little blue then losing consciousness and slowly slithering down her leg. The experience for me was one of a blissful out of body experience similar to kundalini rise I provoke during practice.

As I have lived this life in this body I have experienced and internally observed several different types of natural kundalini events. They are abundant if we observe.

Now, on to the other type of Kundalini Rise.

The other type I call 'unnatural' or more accurately, 'yogically produced' kundalini rises. This kind is voluntarily generated through manipulation of breathing (pranayama), manipulation of the physical body (asana) and internalization of the mind (pratyahara). In the electrical center of the head, the core-self (atma) is awake and alert. It objectively wants to pull the kundalini in a controlled fashion up into itself and then move that same life force into places throughout the psyche. Once a kundalini exercise session is completed the core-self has the great opportunity to practice meditation with the goal of and possibility for, self-realization.

For the first many years of my yoga practice I did not have the proper instruction. I was not performing breath infusion in my postures. During postures I would occasionally have kundalini rises that were unplanned and they involved a painful pounding of energy moving through my head. I did not know at the time it was because contaminated energy was being forced up my spine as I had not properly replaced the carbon dioxide in my system with oxygen. Incorporating breath infusion (bhastrika) into the asana solved this problem.

During a kundalini yoga session we are not listening to music or stimulating the senses. In fact, we aim to greatly decrease sensual stimuli and work to detoxify the subtle body and its parts. We make great efforts to extract burdensome sensual energies out of the system, making way for a meaningful, supremely enjoyable, safely and thoroughly executed kundalini rise.

So what's in a kundalini rise?

Are they all the same?

How do we gauge their meaning and their effectiveness in regard to our spiritual practice? Not so much in regard to our material lives and how much pleasure we are trying to experience, but how does it apply to our spiritual practice, how does it benefit it?

Can the overuse of the natural types of kundalini activation actually contribute to our attachments here?

Does the purposeful (yogic) kundalini rise aid us in reaching transcendental places and people in order to ultimately relocate to a heavenly world – a world free of anxiety?

What does kundalini yoga mean to you really?

Is it just a rush? Or is it a means to an end?

Is it a turban and some mantras or is it the core-self as a hacker, going into rewrite part of a set program?

To me the difference between the natural and the unnatural Yoga driven rise is the difference between a gun shot, and an atom bomb.

One is a quick shot; it's nice and satisfying on a surface level. It is easy to achieve but its effects are redundant and short-lived.

The other is profound, difficult to make and tricky to manage. It has lasting, life changing effects. It has the power to change the current environment.

32
Face to Face with Kundalini: Psychedelic Yoga (No Drugs Necessary)

Do you know what it is to yogically raise kundalini?

Have you had the experience?

It happens during an exercise session.

For experienced students it is planned and prepared for. For new students still learning to handle the energy it can sometimes happen unexpectedly.

Yogic exercises, no matter what name they go by, are meant to produce what can be thought of as a *yogically*-induced-psychedelic-experience.

What's that?

And is your yoga teacher moving you toward this experience?

Kundalini is the Sanskrit word for the subtle but super dynamic life-force energy that animates and functions the physical body and concentrates at the base of the spine near the genitals in a coiled formation. It is this energy which is comprehensively enhanced through the yoga exercises and breathing resulting in cleanliness of energy (purification) and the ability to fulfill yoga meditation stages. (Patanjali's stages 6-8 found in the Yoga Sutras)

During certain asana, combined with aggressive breathing, breath retention and the yogic locks (bhandas), a transcendental event can occur wherein energies (kundalini) of your body travel upward into the head causing feelings of great euphoria, tingling transcendence of consciousness to another state that may consist of colorful awareness of inner lights, living mandalas, blissful sensations and a direct experience of the supernatural material electricity's one lives within.

Young students upon being directed through this process most often *faint*.

Yes, faint.

Hatha Yoga, as explained by Swatmarama in the Pradipika, is super serious and is not a glorified stretch session as seen in most so called yoga classes.

Hatha Yoga is otherworldly.

I never teach a yoga class anymore without first teaching the yogic locks, or bhandas, which align the spine and centralize core consciousness. *Without the locks we are not practicing hatha yoga.* An entire chapter of the Hatha Yoga Pradipika explains their importance.

Without the locks we cannot be in a physical, much less psychic position, to handle the movement and power of the yogically enhanced life force (kundalini).

Since kundalini can arise spontaneously especially when moving from one asana to another, *all students* need to be equipped with the locks in order to protect themselves from unnecessary falling down.

Application of the locks will help keep one's consciousness in the location of the body so that it can be controlled during the kundalini event.

We are working on managing multiple dimensional levels at once, this is the way of the yogi/yogini.

In class, when it is time for kundalini provoking postures I *assist one student one at a time* until they are able to manage the kundalini rise on their own.

I don't take chances with students and don't teach them half ass yoga so that I don't have to do much work or understand what yoga really is.

Being a yoga teacher, a real yoga teacher unafraid of provoking students energies, is an enormous responsibility and should only be done by those prepared for what can happen.

I've had several students lose consciousness as I hold their collapsing body, often supporting their weight as I lower them to sitting, kneeling or lying, pushing inward their chin lock, whispering in their ear to lock the mind and to stay conscious of where their body is. My teacher has done this for me too.

Occasionally as a student returns to the body, tears stream from their eyes as they integrate the realization that their body contains within it a power that they just came face to face with.

It's called Direct Experience.

Realizing the power contained in your very own presence is deeply revolutionary to one's consciousness and can cause profound existential feelings.

True yogins, those courageous students, willing and ready to produce their own psychedelic experience through the yogic use of oxygen infusion, carbon dioxide release (pranayama), special positioning of the body (asana) and centralized in-self focus (pratyahara), become unafraid of the true nature of their own psyche and are ready to work with the experience again and again.

Kundalini comes up at other times in our lives.

Naturally.

We feel it.

A morning stretch, orgasms, roller coaster rides, sneezing, urinating, the chills, asmr, etc...kundalini does make its way up the body on a fairly regular basis. *But on its own terms.*

Hatha Yoga or kundalini manipulation yoga is not natural in that same way. Kundalini doesn't choose this, it is chosen for it. This decision is on the part of the spiritual self and is the reason that yoga is a *discipline.* The self must contend with our own basic nature.

Yet even though yogic kundalini raising is an obscure function present in nature, *it's not meant for everyone.*

Time and experience will make one intuitively ready for the practice. It really depends on your spiritual type and developmental stage.

We **shouldn't** push people who are not ready.

It can hurt or scare them.

They are not yoga students yet.

That is perfectly ok.

We **should** gently push students we sense are ready.

This takes advanced insight on the part of the teacher.

The bottom line is that most yoga teachers are not teaching hatha yoga properly. Most haven't studied the Pradipika much less use it for class curriculum.

Not even close.

Is your yoga teacher ready for your kundalini rise?

Is he/she promoting it? Explaining it?

Does she/he perform this fundamental yoga function on their own during their own practice?

Ask them! Ask questions in class!

It's time we expect more from Yoga teachers and understanding and respecting kundalini is a good start.

33
Spiritual Liberation = Kundalini Annihilation

In Yoga what we ultimately want is to liberate ourselves from the wheel of reincarnation. The wheel of reincarnation is made of a substance, a bio-psychic material intelligence that, for the purposes of this article, will be known as the 'kundalini life force'.

Kundalini is a Sanskrit word that literally means 'coiled she-serpent'. It is the designation, or name of, the ever changing program we experience and refer to as "Mother Nature". She has many names; some call her Goddess, Madre, the Matrix, the Material Universe, Prakriti.

Kundalini energy is not spiritual energy - quite the contrary!

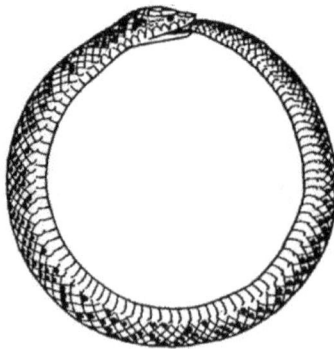

This image represents what this material world is in its simplest principle - a cyclic material force that gives birth to, evolves and simultaneously destroys itself at once. It is not you. You are not it.

We, as spiritual beings, live inside this and we lose track of our identity. We were 'put' into it, so to speak, long ago and it is a closed system with few escape possibilities. Like a womb.

Yoga is an escape possibility.

When we practice yoga we are practicing toward the end of rebirth, this is what our consciousness is focused on, the eventual end of material rebirth, even if it takes a thousand lives practicing yoga, the end of kundalini.

This article will explore my answers to these questions:

What is Kundalini?

How did we get here inside it?

Why should I convince my Kundalini to annihilate itself?

Who am I without it?

What is Kundalini?

Kundalini is the environment in which we live. We call her Mother Nature and when we examine the situation we are in here, we must come to terms with the reality that we are dependents. We are not in charge; we do not run the functions. She manages everything. The body and mind you use belong to her. You do have a personal will of your own but as you might imagine, while you are living with your mother, it is her will that dominates in her house.

In this case, on a universal scale, she is the generator, organizer and dispenser (the g.o.d) of our current reality.

But let me ask you this. Do you want to live with your mother forever? Isn't it a natural progression of one's development to eventually move out, move on and become one's own person, no longer singularly identifying with mother's energy? Through lifetimes of birth and death we learn to appreciate, admire and respect our mother, but do we want to live under her authority and sensual requirements eternally?

Or? Do we think more of ourselves and our own personal spiritual identity and ability to mature out from under mom's excessive control? In Yoga we do think more of ourselves and want to know more about ourselves and the other side of existence.

Remember, the mystic nature of the serpent has been revered, feared and worshipped throughout all recorded time. Why? My guess is that once human intelligence evolved the intelligence to notice the similarity between the serpent and the human spine/chakra complex they put two and two together and discovered a way to symbolize and honor the Earth, the elements and the universe.

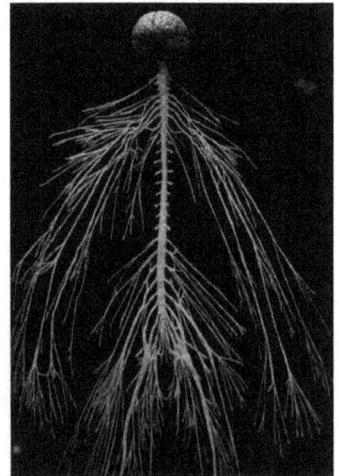

The human spine, epitome of evolutionary progress, walks around like an upright, confident serpent who has sprouted (evolved) a head and arms and legs and an extravagant nervous system. It loves, and is programmed to think, it is somebody.

Look at the central serpent that is the spine.

How did we get inside it?

So how did we get here and how did the evolutionary process begin?

Through meditation I have come to understand that this natural universe, including all its corresponding astral planes, is an incubator kind of structure and we were put here through the divine, yet causeless, interaction between spiritual energy and material energy – between mom and dad.

The supreme Mother and Father, attracted to one another, capable of interaction and creation, but independent of each other as well.

They came into contact and He ejaculated us into her and here we are.

What science calls the big bang, I call the *Big Ejaculate*.

The meeting of the grand masculine and grand feminine produces a strange world and is most accurately symbolized by the Shiva Lingham and Durga Yoni in Hinduism, as shown.

It took me much time in meditation to understand the deep importance of this combination.

We spiritually originate in the Father energy because He is stable, unaffected and all spiritual energy originates in Him.

Everything that is material is of Her, the Mother energy, she is unstable, affected. All *particles*, subtle and physical, originate in her.

It's true that in reality each of us, as real beings, is an eternal nano-spark of spiritual energy - but we can't deny that we live in a material environment and that it is what we relate to most. It is the sole source of our anxiety and lack of understanding ourselves.

In yoga we aim to conquer that misidentification that causes perpetual anxiety and discipline ourselves out of confusion and misunderstanding.

How?

If we are into Yoga here's how -

- Patanjali's 8 steps of Yoga found in the Yoga Sutras- here we find that we are expected to clean up the materialistic life through lifestyle regulations, obligations, also through mystic exercises, purification breathing, internalization of attention energies, and the three stage meditation process beginning with effortful connection to a higher concentration source, then to spontaneous less effortful connection, and then into a consciousness of complete insight (samadhi).

- In yoga we believe we have to cultivate a lack of interest in the mundane physical/psychic world and focus our efforts off the physical/mental grid and relocate our conscious attention toward association with higher forces and beings of spiritual energy through an advanced type of dissociative meditation called samyam which is stages 6, 7, and 8 of the Patanjali yoga process. See Chapter 1 Verses 12-17 of The Yoga Sutras, translation by Michael Beloved

- Study and practice of The Bhagavad Gita

- Study and practice of the Hatha Yoga Pradipika.

Why should I convince my Kundalini to annihilate itself?

The ultimate answer to that question is, because it's worth it.

During meditation I have felt and experienced more than mere glimpses of the spiritual world. The feeling of proper spiritual identification is life changing.

What we want, as yogins, is to pull ourselves up, brush off the dust that is the kundalini sense suit, and start our spiritual lives in earnest, heading toward an environment suitable to the heart of the spiritual being.

Who Am I Without It?

Through my practice, supported by the guidance of my teacher, I've proven to myself that I am separate from the kundalini life force and that I possess a spiritual will.

This will is the force of who I am as a spiritual person (atma) and it has to work hard, day and night to maintain any kind relationship or awareness with itself while existing in this universe. This universe is a total distraction to spiritual living, but is also the only way out. We must harness these material energies and make them work for, serve and even adore the core-self.

It is the greatest hope I have ever felt.

The proof to myself that I am me.

That I exist….and possess a will that can do things in this world! I can assert myself and act contrary to the sensual desires of kundalini!

I can reform the nature of the body and mind I use.

This will has the power to reform the body mind to the point where the body/mind accepts that it is not eternal, accepts that it is but a tiny, deteriorating reflection of what the glorious self really is. It finds this out in meditation. It accepts that it is insufficient as a self and that it cannot be alone, the self. It realizes that it is the spiritual self and it will not be lost if the kundalini annihilates.

Everything that is wondrous about you, everything worth holding onto exists in the spirit.

Nothing is lost, when all this is gone.

Conclusion

Thank you for reading my book, *Splitting the Atma: Revelations on Yoga*. My adoration and devotion to the study of this wonderful practice is encapsulated in this and my other publications. There is nothing I enjoy writing about more, or talking about or defending as much as I do Yoga.

My journey of reincarnation has been so influenced by the appearance of Yoga in this, and past lives. I have memories of my most recent past life in the early 1900's as author/teacher Ida Craddock, who, once again, wrote on Yoga especially as it pertained to sex reformation and the potential joys of the marital union. I invest a lot of time with Yoga - the kind of time many people invest in socializing, or traveling, or partying, or building a career. I've sacrificed (some may say neglected) certain natural aspects of life for the sake of the pleasure experienced when grasping the spiritual promises and profundities of the psychological Yoga system.

I wholeheartedly believe that for those with the interest in existential things, time spent contemplating, studying, practicing, discussing matters of divinity, reincarnation, self-hood, spirituality, destiny and all types of philosophy, is time very well spent.

Best of fortunes to you traveler, as you journey onward and upward toward your greatest expression of self.

About the Author

Erinn Earth (devaPriya Yogini) is a Yoga Educator, former social worker, current licensed cosmetologist, musician and mother to a grown son.

After graduating from Quincy University in 1996 with a degree in Psychology, Erinn discovered Yoga as the greatest of humanities psychological studies. Practicing the 8 steps of yoga shed a bright light on the nature of existence and inspired a deeper understanding of her-self. As a means to this end, yoga continues to equip Erinn with mystic techniques (kriyas) which provide continuous, aggressive purification of the ever self-contaminating psyche, as well as healing relief to the physical body.

Erinn discovered that philosophical study of the Yoga Sutras, Bhagavad Gita and Hatha Yoga Pradipika, as well as yogic exercises, breathing and meditation caused a brilliant reform of consciousness- a much needed opportunity to sort her-self out.

Erinn was born in 1974 and grew up an adoptee in a rural Illinois Catholic family. She started singing and playing guitar as a child. She has lived near the sea in sunny Florida for 10 years.

Yoga teaching began in 2000 after formal training at the Sivananda Ashram in the Laurentian Mountains of Quebec. There, Erinn lived in a tent and studied with monks. She conscientiously engaged in yoga austerities, fully cooperative with the requirements of study and controlled lifestyle. This is where she learned the sacred discipline of Kirtan chanting that she shares with students and friends.

In 2013 Erinn met inSelf Yoga™ master, Michael Beloved and received training in breath infusion for subtle body transformation, a form of kundalini hatha yoga. She has received two inSelf Yoga™ certifications and continues teaching under his guidance.

Yoga is an ancient science of introspection, psychological purification and ultimate, effortless togetherness with the Supreme Person through meditation.

Publications

Core-Self Discovery

This guided meditation, narrated by devaPriya, is available on DVD and in book form for easy carry along.

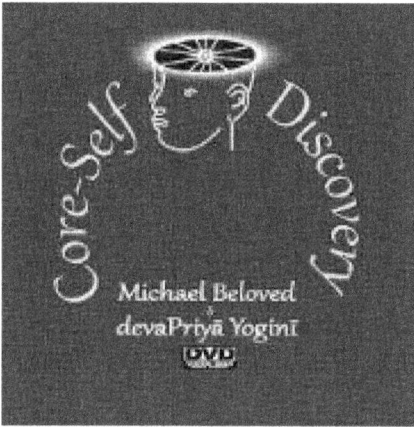

This is the pictorial format of the inSelf Yoga® course for discovering the core-self in the psyche of the individual soul. This was adapted from Michael Beloved's "Meditation Pictorial" book.

The mind diagrams give graphic depiction of what should take place in the head of the subtle body during meditations for pinpointing the core-self, the observing transcendental I-identity.

If you do not have a teacher, then perhaps with this information you will not require one. This is book-guru. No need to run to a seminar here, a workshop there, a trip to exotic India or even a retreat in Colorado. At your leisure, anywhere anytime, this book-guru is available to you. Available online or by request:

Kundalini Yoga Home Practice

Erinn's fully illustrated booklet offers clarifying information on:

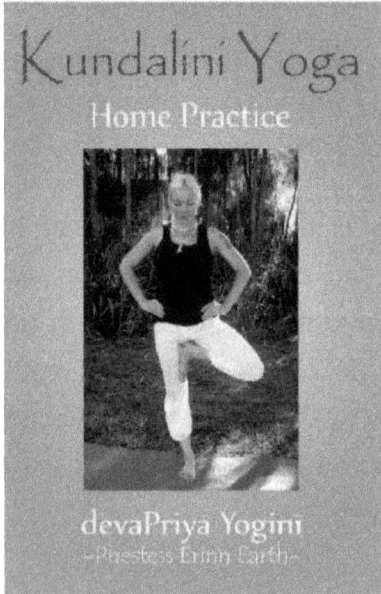

Kundalini Yoga
Home Practice

devaPriya Yogini
~Priestess Erinn Earth~

-Yoga's 8 Steps
-The nature of Kundalini
-Self-supervising a 5 part kundalini session for subtle body transformation including details on sensual interest retraction (Pratyahara)
-Advanced breath infusion (Bhastrika)
-Overcoming troublesome functions of mind
-Detecting the supernatural Naad sound as a source of concentration during meditation.

This book is a summary and an elaboration on the topics discussed in Erinn's group classes. Yoga classes can be opportunity for teachers to mystically transmit techniques to a few students at once. The student then takes the technique home and uses it to develop insight. Using the practice booklet as a reference for home practice, the student can then return to class prepared to receive another technique.

Sun Gazing, Aura Seeing & Naad Hearing: Exercises for Increased Psychic Sensitivity

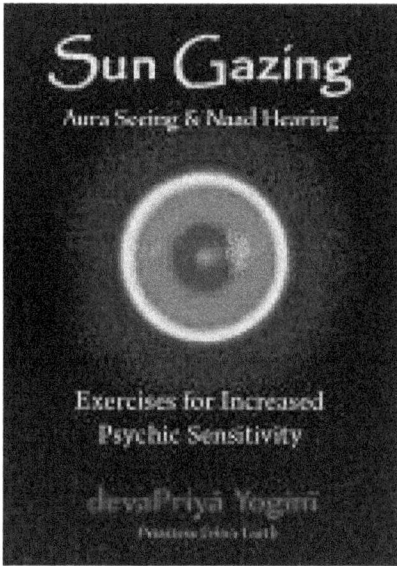

This book offers intense insight into the study of light, the study of auras & the deeply mystic practice of naad sound listening. Erinn's (devaPriya's) personal experience is interwoven into this partially autobiographical book, along with techniques for increasing subtle sensitivity.

Descriptive and instructional, even if you have not done exercises for increasing this type of awareness in the past, but have an interest to try, this would be a useful text. Sun Gazing is a multi-dimensional practice with many facets discovered by Erinn and certainly many mystics drawn toward sun study. Sun Gazing certainly is not reduced to senselessly staring at the sun.

Online Resources

Website: http://inselfyoga.net

Forum: http://inselfyoga.com

Email: erinnearth@yahoo.com

www.ingramcontent.com/pod-product-compliance
Lightning Source LLC
LaVergne TN
LVHW041250080426
835510LV00009B/678